P. A. B. WIDENER
Dean of Philadelphia's Rapid Transit
Director Philadelphia Rapid Transit Company

Philadelphia's Rapid Transit

BEING AN ACCOUNT

of the *Construction* and *Equipment* of the

MARKET STREET SUBWAY-ELEVATED

and its place in the great system and
service of the Philadelphia Rapid
Transit Company

Together with

A review of the work of the
Millard Construction Co.

BY

Philadelphia Rapid
Transit Company

PHILADELPHIA, PA., U.S.A.
MCMVIII

Entered with the Librarian of Congress
at Washington, September, 1908, by
Arnold & Dyer, Philadelphia

©2008-2010 Periscope Film LLC
All Rights Reserved
ISBN#978-1-935700-26-5
www.PeriscopeFilm.com

ARNOLD & DYER
PHILADELPHIA

INTRODUCTION

THE City of Philadelphia is proud of her sub-title the "City of Homes;" but the very fact that every workingman has his separate home in this city resulted in such a scattering of the population as made the expenditure necessary for an elevated or subway road a very doubtful enterprise from the investors' point of view. New York, Boston and Chicago, with their apartment houses for the rich and tenement houses for the poor, gave a tributary population along the main arteries of travel which would easily support such lines, and Philadelphia was therefore the last of the great cities to attain elevated and subway transportation. But while she was the last to get it, she was the first in which the subways were built by private capital, and she has profited by the experience and mistakes of other cities, and to-day presents the finest specimen of elevated and subway construction in the world.

The topography of Philadelphia was such that its surface travel has been taken care of by a perfect network of tracks, aggregating over 600 miles in length, so that throughout the central part of the city every 400 feet finds a street occupied by a street railway track. The streets are narrow, and with a grade crossing every 400 feet, the rate at which cars could be safely moved was necessarily slower than prevailed in other cities. Many "L" lines had been established in order to take the public directly from their homes to their places of business without change of cars, and the result was a congestion of travel in the central portion of the city, which cried for remedy.

The controlling interests of the Union Traction Company which, by a series of combinations extending over a period of 20 years, had come into control of all the surface lines, recognized that something had to be done, even though the expenditure required would not be at once productive of an attractive revenue. And accordingly in 1902 they acquired the franchise previously granted for an elevated road the length of Market Street.

It will be recalled that this franchise was for an elevated road and not a subway. With the interests of the city placed ahead of their own financial interests, the Union Traction Company management first secured an amendment of this franchise so as to permit the building of the subway between the two rivers, and, secondly, secured a further amendment under which they were allowed to construct their portals upon private property, that at the east end being acquired by the new Company at a cost of upwards of half a million dollars, and that at the west end requiring the construction of a separate bridge over the Schuylkill River. While, therefore, the enterprise, as originally conceived, was of doubtful success from a financial standpoint, these people, whom it is popular to think of only as looking after their own interests, took upon themselves an additional expenditure of several million dollars solely for the best interests of the City of Philadelphia. The work is now completed; it is a monument to the unselfish public spirit of the financial interests which attempted it, to the skill of the engineers who designed it and the contractors who built it, under difficulties never before encountered in similar work. Whether it will pay directly is a question yet to be determined. If, however, it should bring to the management of the present operating Company, the Philadelphia Rapid Transit Company, some recognition from the public that their interests are first considered, it will at once prove a profitable investment.

OUTLINE OF THE MARKET STREET SUBWAY-ELEVATED

THE Market Street Elevated Passenger Railway extends from a terminal at Sixty-ninth Street, west of the city boundary in Delaware County, on an east and west line to the ferries on the Delaware River. It comprises one of several routes of rapid transit railways for which franchises were granted by Councils of the City of Philadelphia in 1901. The Market Street line, and a short section of the Frankford Elevated Railway, which is used as the eastern terminal of the Market Street line, are the only routes utilized up to this time. By ordinance of Councils in 1902 a subway was authorized between the Schuylkill and Delaware Rivers.

At the Sixty-ninth Street terminal is located a passenger station connecting the Market Street line with electric lines that tap portions of Delaware, Montgomery, and Chester Counties, also the repair shops, a power house, sidings, storage yards, and other appurtenances for the maintenance of the line.

The first section of the railway runs on private property in cut and fill, with retaining walls, to the Millbourne Mills, near Cobb's Creek, immediately west of the city line. Thence the route is by two-track elevated structure in the centre of Market Street to the new bridge built by the Company over the Schuylkill River.

The Schuylkill River Bridge is located 100 feet north of the centre line of Market Street. It is reached by reverse curves on the Elevated Railway from the west, and connects by reverse curves and an incline with the Subway running east under the bed of Market Street to the City Hall and the Delaware River.

The Bridge and the Subway as far as the City Hall have four tracks, the two inner tracks for trains operating on the Elevated Railway, and the two outer tracks for the surface cars from West Philadelphia. At the City Hall the tracks diverge, the two eastbound and the two westbound passing to the south and north of the City Hall respectively. The tracks for the surface cars terminate in a loop on the east side of the City Hall, passing under the through tracks, so that all street cars from West Philadelphia return westward after passing around the City Hall.

The two tracks for trains continue on the East Market Street Subway to Front Street; thence north by curve and an incline on private property between Front and Water Streets, and then by Elevated Railway on Arch Street to Delaware Avenue, proceeding south on Delaware Avenue to the eastern terminus at South Street. The Delaware River ferries at Market, Chestnut, and South Streets have stations on the Delaware Avenue Elevated.

A third rail supplies power for the Elevated and Subway trains; the cars that enter the Subway from the surface lines are operated by overhead trolley.

With the completion of the east section of the Subway by the Millard Construction Company, the line was practically finished. It was thrown open to public travel from Sixty-ninth Street to the Second Street station on August 3, 1908, having been open as far as Fifteenth Street for some months. The Delaware Avenue section was then rapidly nearing completion.

	Location	No. of Tracks	Lineal Feet of Structure	Lineal Feet of Single Track
Section No. 12 Cut, fill and retaining walls	West terminal to Millbourne Mills	2	2,292	4,584
Section No. 2-A Steel elevated structure with open floor	Millbourne Mills to Sixty-third Street	2	680	1,360
Section No. 2 Steel elevated structure with solid floor	Sixty-third Street to Schuylkill River Bridge	2	18,697	37,394
Section No. 1 Riveted lattice bridge	Schuylkill River Bridge	4	576	2,304
Section No. 4 Open incline and subway	West house line Twenty-second Street to Schuylkill River Bridge	4 (Sub.) 4 (Inc.)	452 267	2,876
Section No. 3 Subway	Fifteenth Street to Twenty-second Street	4	3,243	12,972
Section No. 3-A Subway	Fifteenth Street to W. Broad Street	4	173	692
Section No. 5 Subway	About City Hall	2 (each side)	2,139	4,769
Section No. 5-A Subway	40 lineal feet east of Juniper Street	2	40	80
Section No. 6 Subway	From 40 feet east of Juniper Street to the east portal	2	5,889	11,778
Section No. 7 Open incline with concrete viaduct and retaining walls	East portal to Arch and Water Streets	2	498	996
Section No. 11 Steel elevated structure	Arch and Water Streets by Delaware Avenue to South Street	2	403 open floor 3,758 solid floor	806 10,167
			39,107 7.41 miles	90,778 17.20 miles.

4

The preceding tabulated statement, giving the kind and number of lineal feet of structure, number of tracks, and lineal feet of single track, is of interest as summarizing the whole line. The section numbers show how the construction work was divided up for ease of working.

The railway is located on right of way purchased by the Company from the eastern boundary of the Sixty-ninth Street Terminal to the abutment near the Millbourne Mills. This part of the line comprises about 720 lineal feet of fill between retaining walls. It includes a reinforced concrete bridge which forms the outlet for a lane. The remainder consists of grading on a side hill sloping downward to the north toward Cobb's Creek, and to the dam furnishing water-power to the Millbourne Mills. The southerly side of the roadbed for considerable distance is flanked by a retaining wall. The total length of this section is 2,292 feet.

A passenger station has been built near the line of Sixty-sixth Street, to serve a new settlement known as Millbourne, between the railway and the West Chester Pike. A frame station has been erected with stairways and bridging for access to the east and west bound platforms over the tracks.

Considerable work was required for the drainage of the sloping territory on the south of the line. Paved gutters were made at the base of the slope, discharging into iron pipes that cross under the tracks to the waterway on the north.

This section of the work was built between May 25, 1905, and December 3, 1906, including some additional walls about the Sixty-sixth Street station, not contemplated at the time the work was started.

The alignment is half on curve and half on tangent. One tangent extends past the Sixty-sixth Street station, the sharpest curve having a radius of 500 feet on the centre line of the roadbed. The line ascends from the western end of the section to the east 23 feet in the entire length, the maximum grade being 2.84 per cent.

The principal items of construction on the section total as follows:

```
Excavation ................................................ 12,048 cubic yards
Stone masonry.............................................. 7,759 cubic yards
Concrete .................................................... 355 cubic yards
Reinforcing rods for concrete ............................... 9 tons
Iron fence .................................................. 3,594 lineal feet
Earth fill .................................................. 5,098 cubic yards
```

In the East Market Street Subway the passenger platforms at the stations are all on tangent. They are 350 feet long—except at the Thirteenth Street station, where they are 364 feet long—and provide for eight-car trains. The clear space between the edges of the platforms and the sides of the cars is 3 inches, and the platforms are 3 feet 6 inches above the tops of the rails. The edges of the platforms and the steps on all stairways are provided with carborundum safety treads to prevent slipping.

All stairways leading to the street are 5 feet 8 inches wide between side walls, and are surmounted by iron hoods of ornamental design.

Each of the stations has ample exits and entrances. At Second Street there are eight openings to the sidewalks. Four are used as entrances and four as exits. At Fifth Street there are two openings on Fifth Street just south of Market Street, and four openings on Market Street just west of Fifth Street, with one opening through the property, 433 Market Street. At Eighth Street there is an opening on the street in front of the property 730 Market Street. The other entrances and exits are through the various department stores at the corner of Eighth and Market Streets. Eleventh Street has seven openings on the street, with entrances and exits through the buildings at the corners. Thirteenth Street has six entrances and exits to the street, and two through a department store. All the entrances and exits through department stores and other buildings are open day and night.

West of the City Hall there are only two stations in the Subway—Fifteenth Street and Nineteenth Street. The latter is served by the Subway-Surface line cars only, the Subway-Elevated cars not stopping until the Schuylkill is crossed and the Elevated station at Thirty-second Street is reached.

The keynote of the Subway station design is a massive simplicity, in harmony with the dignity peculiar to the concrete of which they are built.

But at Eighth, Eleventh, and Thirteenth Streets the department stores and other buildings have introduced a brilliant note by providing handsome entrances to their respective establishments and long series of show windows, as attractively dressed and brightly lighted as those on the main street level. The windows are on the main platform level at Thirteenth Street, while at Eleventh Street they stretch along the 300 foot concrete balconies above the main platform.

Eighth Street is the show point, with its numerous department stores, aggregating several hundred feet of brilliantly lighted show windows, and its store entrances, rich in marble and tiling and polished wood and artistic metal work. By the cross-over from balcony to balcony above the roofs of the trains, the shopper can go from building to building without stepping on to the street. Each of the store entrances has one or more ticket offices, designed in harmony with its immediate surroundings.

Each station is provided with four toilet rooms, two on each platform. The toilet rooms are furnished with modern sanitary fixtures, the floors and wainscoting lined with mosaic ceramic tiles. To provide for ventilating the toilets, General Electric 550 volt electric fans have been installed, each expelling 460 cubic feet of air per minute through special ventilating ducts. All of the fixtures in the toilet rooms are

JOHN B. PARSONS
President Philadelphia Rapid Transit Company

vented in accordance with the best practice, the vents leading to the sidewalk, into which gratings are placed.

The ticket booths in the stations on East Market Street are built of brick to the level of the counters, the brick being faced with mosaic ceramic tiles. The counters, the facing and the cornice are of Italian marble. The ticket booths at the Second, Fifth, and Eighth Streets stations are placed in the middle of the stations under the cross streets, in bays or extensions designed in the Subway structure. The booths on the north side of the Eleventh and Thirteenth Streets stations are also placed in the middle of the stations, while those on the south side of these stations are located in the southeast corners of the lobbies in bays or extensions of the Subway proper.

The running time from Sixty-ninth Street to Second Street is twenty-seven minutes eastward; westward the heavy grades add one minute to the time. Between the City Hall and Second Street the running time is seven minutes, or less than half the best time possible on the surface lines.

Surface-Subway cars, coming on to the Market Street surface tracks from the Woodland Avenue, Lancaster Avenue, Baring Street, and Angora lines at Thirty-second Street, cross the Schuylkill River and run through the western section of the Subway. They occupy the extreme north and south tracks of the four in this section, stopping at Nineteenth Street and Fifteenth Street. They then loop around the City Hall on tracks below the main Subway tracks, stopping at a lower level platform at Thirteenth Street station to take on westbound passengers. Passengers from this line desiring to go east are transferred to the Subway trains at Fifteenth Street station.

Owing to the fact that the different rapid transit lines as contemplated radiated like the ribs of a fan from the eastern portion of Market Street, it was impossible to arrange for suitable common shops or terminals on the eastern end. The Philadelphia Rapid Transit Company, therefore, purchased a tract of about thirty acres lying just west of the city line, near Sixty-ninth Street, and has built on this property an Inspection Barn, Storage Yards, Repair Shops, also a large Terminal Building, which serves to make easy the transfer of passengers from the trains of the Philadelphia Rapid Transit Company to the cars of the Philadelphia & West Chester Traction Company, Philadelphia & Western Railroad Company, or any other lines which might radiate from that point. The storage yard will have an ultimate capacity of two hundred cars. The inspection barn will hold four trains of cars at one time, and this, as well as the shops themselves, has been designed with the idea of future extension whenever required.

Both shops and inspection barn are built with brick walls, concrete roof resting on iron trusses, concrete floors, and with pits under all tracks. The floor in the inspection barn is dropped twelve inches below the head of the rail. The shops are built along both sides of a transfer table running approximately north and south. The shop on the west of the table is used for car washing, jacking-up the bodies, overhauling the trucks, machine shop and blacksmith shop; the shops on the east side of the transfer table contain the paint shops, storage facilities, etc. The transfer table, instead of running on four to six tracks, has only two, the table consisting of two plate girders of 45 foot span, carrying the tracks and platform for the motor and controller. The table operates in a pit 5 feet deep, at one side of which is a tunnel through which wires, heating pipes, etc., are laid. The shops and inspection barn are all heated and lighted from a small power plant containing two 250 horse-power B. & W. boilers, two Fitchburg compound condensing engines, and Westinghouse 3 wire 220 volt generators. The power plant also contains a 75 kilowatt DeLaval turbo-generator set for day use, and the duplex air compressor used to supply the signal system and air tools in the shops.

Passenger accommodations of the Terminal are very complete and efficient. The trains of the Philadelphia Rapid Transit Company run through on depressed tracks, separate platforms being used for incoming and outgoing passengers. The main floor of the Terminal, on which are located the general waiting room and lobby, is somewhat above the street level and connects with the depressed tracks by easy stairways. Adjoining this room on the west, and on the same level, is the terminal of the Delaware County trolley lines to West Chester, Ardmore, and Collingdale; and wide corridors running north give access to the cars of the Philadelphia & Western Railroad. Toilets and other accommodations for travellers are of the latest approved style. On the upper floors of the building are the rooms for trainmen and motormen, and for the operating officials of the division.

The building is of brick and reinforced concrete, of dignified and substantial design, well suited to express the purpose for which it was built.

GEORGE D. WIDENER
First Vice-President Philadelphia Rapid Transit Company

GENERATION AND DISTRIBUTION OF POWER

IN the year 1902, when the Philadelphia Rapid Transit Company leased the Union Traction Company, it found that Company operating several power generating plants, most of which had been built by the underlying companies.

Direct current only was generated in all these plants, at a potential of 525 to 575 volts. To supply some of the feeders to outlying districts "boosters" were in use.

The plants were located as follows:

No. 1.	7500 kilowatts	Thirteenth and Mt. Vernon Streets	Philadelphia Traction Company.
No. 4.	6000 kilowatts	Thirty-third and Market Streets	
No. 5.	2100 kilowatts	Thirty-second and Dauphin Streets	
No. 2.	3700 kilowatts	920 North Delaware Avenue	Electric Traction Company.
No. 6.	1700 kilowatts	Twenty-seventh and South Streets	
No. 3.	5000 kilowatts	Beach and Green Streets	Peoples Traction Company.
No. 7.	2900 kilowatts	Ogontz	
No. 8.	500 kilowatts	Chestnut Hill	Union Traction Company.
No. 9.	1500 kilowatts	Willow Grove	
No. 10.	400 kilowatts	Second and Wyoming Avenue	

Total, 31,300 kilowatts.

It was evident that all the future development of the city must be in the suburban or outer sections, too distant to be taken care of by the existing plants. Also it was realized that the large amount of power required to operate the 115 miles of elevated and subway railways, then proposed, would require either that new direct current plants be built in outlying districts and the older stations be modernized and enlarged, or that a large central station be built and equipped with more modern type of machinery, generating high tension, alternating, 3 phase current, and distributing this to substations located along the lines of development.

At these substations the high tension 3 phase current would be transformed to 575 volt direct current and supplied to the surface or rapid transit lines as required.

The latter plan was adopted, and all suitable sites for the necessary buildings were canvassed. The properties purchased near Laurel Street run from Delaware Avenue on the east to Beach Street on the west, 200 feet deep, with 435 feet front on Beach Street and 415 feet front on Delaware Avenue. Adjoining these properties on the south is the old station No. 2, 920 North Delaware Avenue. On the new site is built the first section of the plant. The future sections are to be built on the site of the old plant, which will be replaced by a substation in the Kensington district, and supplied with current from the central plant.

The completed central plant is to contain nine turbo-generators of 6000 kilowatts each (nominal rating). The 3 phase current is generated at 13,200 volts and the entire distribution in the city limits is by underground conduits and lead covered, paper insulated, triple conductor cables.

The first section of the central plant, which is now completed and in operation, contains three Westinghouse turbo-generators, of 6000 kilowatts capacity each. This power is supplied to substations located as follows:

820 Sansom Street	9000 kilowatts	These substations supply current to both surface cars and rapid transit lines.
Fifty-sixth and Market Streets	4500 kilowatts	
Fifty-eighth and Woodland Avenue	3000 kilowatts	These substations supply current to surface cars only.
Fifty-second and Lancaster Avenue	3000 kilowatts	
Thirteenth and Snyder Avenue	3500 kilowatts	

These substations also receive current from the auxiliary power plant at Second and Wyoming Avenue, containing 11,000 kilowatts of 3 phase generating machinery, which has been installed by the Philadelphia Rapid Transit Company since 1902, and which supplies also the following substations:

Frankford and Arrott Streets	2000 kilowatts	These substations supply current to surface cars only.
Chelten Avenue	4500 kilowatts	
Glenside	2000 kilowatts	
Willow Grove	2000 kilowatts	

The Philadelphia Rapid Transit Company now operates 66,000 kilowatts of generating machinery,—an increase of 34,700 kilowatts since 1902, when it acquired the plants of the Union Traction Company. It has also acquired the plants of the Doylestown & Willow Grove and the Darby, Media & Chester Street Railway, by lease of these roads.

A considerable amount of new machinery has been installed in the leased plants during the last six years, the greater part of this increase being for the operation of surface cars.

The street level at the Delaware Avenue power house is about $+8$ feet (city datum). The character of the ground, consisting of about 6 feet of fill, 7 feet of gravel, 12 feet of clay and 20 feet of mud, with a mean high water level of $-2\frac{1}{4}$ feet and a mean low water level of $-8\frac{1}{2}$ feet, necessitated pile foundations.

Concrete piles of the Raymond type were selected, and 920 were set in place, with an average load of 33 tons each. Concrete caps were placed on these piles, which became the footings for concrete piers; these piers being continued up through the basement to the first floor level of the boiler room, from which point the skeleton steel work started and continued to the roof.

The skeleton steel work construction on the engine room side started from the basement, the level of which is city datum, and continued to the roof.

Curtain walls above grade are of red brick laid in red mortar. The arches also are of brick. Terra cotta of the same color as the brick is used for the trimmings, the only architectural adornment being the horizontal bands at the water table, first floor, and cornice levels. This gives a very satisfactory appearance for a power house, owing to the fact that it will not show the dirt as much as some lighter or more contrasting materials.

Dark red "Jewetville" brick is used for the interior of the engine (or turbine) room to the top of the piers. The arches are turned with buff brick, and the terra cotta trims for the arches and the cornice are also buff. Both the red and the buff brick used on the interior are semi-glazed.

Roofs also are of concrete slabs with steel reinforcement. The slabs are supported on steel trusses with tar and gravel roofing.

All windows and skylights have metal frames glazed with wire glass.

The present steam plant of this station consists of two 9000 horse-power single flow and one 9000 horse-power double flow Westinghouse-Parsons steam turbines, each of these machines being capable of developing 50 per cent. above this rating if necessary.

The station is built on the unit principle, each unit containing eight 800 horse-power Parker boilers, which are of the double furnace superheater type. Each furnace is fitted with an 80 square-foot Roney stoker. Each unit of boilers is supplied with a reinforced concrete stack 14 feet in diameter by 175 feet high above the steel base on which it is carried. The stacks are carried on a framework of steel columns and girders spanning the two middle boilers of each unit; the base of the stack being approximately 50 feet above the boiler room floor, and anchored to the steel supporting structure by thirty $2\frac{1}{2}$ inch anchor bolts. A steel breeching carries the waste gases from each unit of boilers up to the base of the stack. At the base of the stack is a special four-part wing damper, which is operated by an automatic damper regulator.

Coal is fed to the boilers from two overhead bunkers extending the entire length of the power house. This method of construction leaves an opening in the centre for the stacks, and also space for light and ventilation. Each bunker has a capacity of 600 tons per generating unit—a total station storage capacity of 1200 tons per unit. There is also an additional storage capacity provided for on the wharf, which, however, is used as a reserve.

The coal handling equipment consists of a system of Webster bucket elevators and scraper conveyors having a normal capacity of about 120 tons per hour, but capable of being operated considerably beyond this rating. One elevator is erected in a steel tower at the north end of the building, and is arranged for taking coal from either the railroad or trolley coal cars, being provided with two receiving hoppers.

The main coal handling equipment, however, is located on Pier No. 41, on the east side of Delaware Avenue. This pier is 400 feet long with an 82 foot front. It contains three railroad tracks. Each track has a reinforced concrete dumping hopper, which, by means of a system of conveyors, delivers the coal to a crusher and then to the elevator, which is operated on a tower at the west end of the pier. The coal is elevated and conveyed across the street on an enclosed bridge about 80 feet above the sidewalk, and delivered to the conveyor system inside the power house. Provision has been made for handling coal from barges as well as from the railroad. A locomotive crane, operated electrically by means of a third rail, is used to unload the barges and deliver coal into a specially designed 14 ton car. It transfers the coal from the crane to the dumping hoppers between the tracks, and thence to the regular coal elevating system. This method of receiving coal is used at present in preference to railroad delivery.

The boiler room floor and foundations are constructed entirely of reinforced concrete, the design being such that the basement is left clear for light and ventilation.

Concrete hoppers are provided to receive the ashes from the stokers. The ashes are drawn out in cars of special design. These are operated over a system of tracks and deliver the ashes into one of two Morse & Williams dumping bucket elevators. These elevators are operated by alternating current motors. They discharge into an elevated reinforced concrete ash bin, the ashes being drawn off from this bin and finally removed by either railroad or trolley car.

The main steam piping is of special soft steel, with Ball & Wood welded steel flanges. The fittings in the main steam piping are made entirely of cast steel, of special design to insure them against any possible damage from strains caused by expansion. The gaskets are of the Government combination type, asbestos and copper. Extra size bolts are used to make the joints. Chapman gate valves and Schutte & Koerting globe and angle valves are used in the main steam piping. These valves are all of special semi-steel, extra heavy pattern, nickel-bronze fitted, and are specially designed for superheated steam.

The main steam header is supported in a gallery at the west end of the boiler room. Connection from each unit of boilers is made to this header by a system of bends to allow for expansion. The header is designed to be continuous only for the first four units, owing to the expansion which must be provided for. This main is allowed to expand in both directions from the centre on roller guides under the main fittings. Connections from this header feed direct to the turbines from above by means of a long bend.

CHARLES O. KRUGER
Second Vice-President and General Manager
Philadelphia Rapid Transit Company

A small auxiliary main is placed in the engine room basement to supply all the auxiliary machinery. All auxiliary piping is lap welded steel pipe, with rolled steel flanges of Vanstone pattern. This main is also constructed on the unit principle, provision being made that steam may always be available from two sources of supply. All steam piping of this plant, both auxiliary and main, is designed to carry 200 pounds steam pressure per square inch at 200° superheat, and in designing the piping, allowance was made to take care of the expansion resulting from this temperature.

Each turbine is connected directly to a Worthington surface condenser having 20,000 square feet of 1 inch composition tubes. It operates on the dry vacuum principle, using a 12 inch by 24 inch by 24 inch Laidlaw-Dunn-Gordon dry vacuum pump. The water of condensation is removed from the condenser and delivered to the feed heater by means of a 5 inch motor-driven Worthington turbine pump. The feed heater for each unit is a 6000 horse-power Hoppes, open type, and is carried on a gallery directly beneath the engine room floor above the boiler feed pump.

The circulating water for the condensers is pumped from the river by means of a 24 inch Worthington volute pump, one pump for each condenser. Each pump is driven by a 14 inch by 14 inch high speed Reeves engine. Two reinforced concrete conduits 5 feet wide by 8 feet high are provided to conduct the water from the river to the building. These intake conduits are made in duplicate and the pumps are provided with duplicate connections to allow for cleaning one conduit at a time without disturbing the operation of the plant. The screens and sluice gates in the conduits are also arranged for cleaning either side independently. The warm water from the condensers is returned to the river by one large reinforced concrete conduit 8 feet by 8 feet, which takes the water and sewage from the entire station.

The general water service for the plant is pumped direct from the river by means of two 10 inch by 14 inch by 12 inch Duplex Scranton steam pumps, one pump being of sufficient size to handle the ordinary requirements of the plant, the other being used as a reserve.

Wherever possible, the auxiliary machinery is steam driven, on account of its reliability and freedom from shut-down in case of mishap to any of the electrical equipment. All the auxiliary machinery is designed to operate with superheated steam, and the exhaust from the same is returned to the feed heater, where it is all utilized in heating the feed water for the boilers. This can readily be done, as no economizers are used. The Parker boiler is of such a design as to lower the flue gases to a point where an economizer would be of little value.

An extensive oil system is provided in connection with the turbine plant. This system has a capacity of 300 barrels of oil. A large storage tank is provided in the upper gallery of the station, and from this point pipe lines supply the main bearings of the turbines. The storage tank is of such a height as to have approximately 20 pounds pressure available at the turbines. The return oil is carried to a large receiving tank, 8 feet by 7 feet by 16 feet. This tank is fitted with a series of baffles and settling compartments to trap out the water and sediment in the oil. Each compartment is provided with an 8 inch pipe by-pass, so arranged that any compartment or all of this tank may be by-passed for repair and cleaning. After passing through this settling tank, the oil is pumped through a system of cooling coils on its way to the storage tank in the upper gallery. The sediment and water collected in the bottom of the settling tank is pumped by an auxiliary pump, and passed through a series of Burt automatic filters, and the filtrate is again pumped into the general oil system. Additional tanks and pumps are provided for receiving new oil and for drawing off old oil from the system, and also for catching any oil which might overflow from the upper storage tank. All pumps are in duplicate.

In addition to the main oil system which supplies the turbines, there is an auxiliary gravity system to supply oil for the auxiliary machinery. This is so arranged that all the oil used in the plant is delivered direct to the machine where it is required.

The entire oil system, both main and auxiliary, is so piped and cross-connected that any part of it may be taken out of service for cleaning or repairs without interfering with the operation of the plant. All screwed joints are made up with litharge and glycerine, and all flanged joints with corrugated lead gaskets.

The water from the feed heaters is pumped into the boilers by means of a 16 inch by 10 inch by 24 inch Scranton Duplex outside packed ram pattern boiler feed pump, one of these pumps being provided for each unit. The pumps are specially designed with piston valves, and adapted to operate under the high steam pressure and superheat. The feed lines are in duplicate and cross-connected in such a manner that any part of the feed system may be repaired without stopping the water supply to the boilers. The large pipes are of extra heavy lap welded pipe, with extra heavy Vanstone flanges; the smaller sizes being extra heavy brass pipe with extra heavy brass fittings.

In addition to the auxiliary machinery already mentioned, two 13 inch by 24 inch by 14 inch Westinghouse direct connected compound engines are used to drive the exciter generators. These are located on the engine room floor between the main generating units, and are operated at high pressure, exhausting into the feed heaters.

Beside the steam driven exciter units, motor driven exciter units are provided, a description of which will be found below.

The following table gives the list of the machines, with sizes, which constitute one generating unit. The station is designed for nine complete units. Two units of the boiler room have been installed complete, and three units of the generating room.

Turbine—Westinghouse-Parsons, 6000 kilowatt.
Condenser—Worthington, 20,000 square feet surface.
Circulating Pump—Worthington, 24 inch volute.
Circulating Pump Engine—Reeves, 14 inch by 14 inch.
Dry Vacuum Pump—Laidlaw-Dunn-Gordon, 12 inch by 24 inch by 24 inch.
Hot Well Pump—Worthington, 5 inch Turbine (motor driven).
Heater—Hoppes open 6000 horse-power. Class R, Form E, 845 square feet.
Boiler Feed Pump—Scranton Duplex Ram, 16 inch by 10 inch by 24 inch.
Boilers—8 Parker Boilers (800 horse-power each), with superheater.
Stokers—16 Roney (80 square feet), 2 per boiler (4 driving engines).
Stacks—Reinforced concrete, 14 feet diameter by 175 feet (225 feet above grate).

The three main generators are of the revolving field Westinghouse type, direct connected to steam turbines, and develop 3 phase 25 cycle alternating current at 13,200 volts.

Each of these generators requires about 200 amperes at 110 volts to excite the rotating field. To supply this excitation there are installed two 150 kilowatt Westinghouse 110 volt direct current generators, direct connected to 240 horse-power Westinghouse compound engines. There are also two 25 kilowatt Westinghouse 110 volt generators, direct connected to 440 volt 3 phase 50 horse-power induction motors. The induction motor generator sets are connected to the 440 volt bus bars through Cutler-Hammer automatic remote controlled starters, and are so arranged that they can be used for exciting the fields of any of the alternators, or to supply current for lighting the building. The wiring of the steam driven exciters is such that their current can be used for exciting the fields of any or all of the alternators, as well as to supply the power for the lighting of the building.

The coal and ash handling apparatus is operated by Westinghouse induction motors, of which there are four 20 and two 25 and three 40 horse-power installed. The power for these is obtained from two sets of transformers, each containing three 200 kilowatt 13,200 volt to 440 volt transformers. These transformers are of the air cooled type, the air for cooling them being furnished by either of two blower outfits, each of which is capable of supplying sufficient air to cool all the six transformers. The blowers are direct connected to $4\frac{1}{2}$ horse-power 440 volt induction motors.

All the alternating current induction motors in this station are connected to a 440 volt bus bar through Cutler-Hammer automatic remote controlled starters, specially designed for this service. As unskilled labor is usually employed for handling the coal and ashes of a power house, it was deemed advisable to make the system of control as simple as possible. The automatic starters are in the basement of the power house. Each is connected with its motor by a 3 phase cable. A ten pair cable connects the control switches with the starters.

The 110 volt control circuit is supplied by the storage batteries used for operating the oil switches. The men operating the coal drag, elevator, crusher, etc., can start or stop any or all of them by simply turning a small snap switch. Most of the motors have two or more points of control. For example, there is a switch at the bottom and another at the top of the coal elevator, and one inside the power house near the short drag for controlling the elevator. As the switches are wired in series, the elevator can only be started from the switch where it is stopped.

The current from the main generators goes through the current transformers, which are set in inverted ducts under the engine room floor, to the generator oil switches; thence to the generator bus bars; and then, by means of either of two selector switches, to the northeast or the northwest main bus. The feeders are grouped together on feeder buses, seven in a group. The feeder buses are connected with either of the main buses by selector oil switches. The generator and selector switches are each rated at 500 amperes per phase. The feeder oil switches are rated at 300 amperes per phase, and the selector switches for the feeder buses are rated at 1200 amperes per phase.

All the oil switches are of the General Electric Type "F," Form H-3, motor operated, remote controlled. The switches for controlling them are on a small bench board placed in front of the instrument board on the switchboard gallery. The operator, from the instruments, has an exact indication of what each generator and feeder circuit is doing, and the switches give him absolute control of these circuits at the same time.

Each generator and feeder circuit is equipped with an overload time-limit relay of the bellows type, as manufactured by the General Electric Company. If an oil switch is opened by the overload relay an alarm is sounded and a lamp lighted, indicating the generator or feeder group.

The power for operating the oil switches is obtained from two storage batteries (one being a reserve) placed in the top gallery. Each battery consists of 56 Type "F," nine plate chloride accumulators, the size of plate being 11 inches by $10\frac{1}{2}$ inches, with a normal discharge rate of 40 amperes for eight hours.

The storage batteries are charged by two Westinghouse 6 kilowatt 125 volt generators, installed on the switchboard gallery. Each is direct connected to a 10 horse-power, 440 volt, 3 phase motor. These generators are so arranged that they may also be operated in parallel with the storage batteries.

The field rheostats of the main generators are placed in the top gallery, and on the side of the face plate is a small 110 volt motor which moves the contact arm on the segments. This motor is controlled from the bench board, and the operator can increase or decrease

ALEXANDER RENNICK
Third Vice-President and Comptroller Philadelphia Rapid Transit
Company

the resistance in series with the field circuit as may be necessary. A small indicating lamp, in front of the switch that controls the rheostat motor, lights momentarily every time the contact passes over a segment. Alongside of the rheostat control switch is the governor control switch. This switch controls the small motor which increases or decreases the tension on the governor spring, varying the amount of the load taken by the turbine.

Power is supplied to the Subway and Elevated from the substations at 820 Sansom Street, and Market and Allison Streets in West Philadelphia.

The Sansom Street substation is a substantial brick building, absolutely fire-proof, with reinforced concrete floors, columns and roof. It is built on the site of the old Philadelphia Traction Company's cable power house.

There are at present installed six 1500 kilowatt Westinghouse 3 phase 25 cycle 250 R. P. M. 600 volt shunt wound rotary converters. The station is laid out to accommodate two additional rotary converters and auxiliary apparatus of the same size.

The voltage is reduced for each of the rotaries by three 550 kilowatt Westinghouse 13,200 volt to 380 volt 25 cycle air blast transformers. The transformers are set directly over an air chamber with a cross-section of 115 square feet. There are two of these air ducts, one on either side of the station, and they are connected by an air chamber of 25 square feet cross-section, built under the basement floor, with a door at each end. The two air chambers can be operated separately or as one by opening the doors.

This station, although built and operated as a unit, may be divided in half and operated as two independent substations, and in case of trouble is sometimes so operated. The two rows of rotary converters are in the centre, and on either side are the air chambers with the transformers, and beyond the transformers are the high tension bus bars. The high tension bus bars are connected together through an oil switch and cables placed in inverted ducts underneath the floor.

Through the centre of the building, running north and south, there are five columns which support the crane runways, one crane spanning the rotary converters and transformers on each side. These cranes are of the 3 motor type, with 25 tons capacity. They span 26 feet $1\frac{1}{2}$ inches. Over the bus bars on each side there is a single "I" beam crane, with a standard Yale & Towne 1-ton Triplex trolley block.

The air for cooling the transformers is supplied by three 90 inch American blower fans. Each has a capacity of 20,000 cubic feet of air per minute at one ounce pressure on continuous duty. These fans are driven by 380 volt 3 phase 25 cycle $17\frac{1}{2}$ horse-power induction motors, and are so arranged that any one or all of them can be run from the transformers of any rotary converter that may be in service.

Only the positive cables of the rotary converter are taken to the switchboard. The negative cables go to a pedestal switch placed alongside the rotary, and thence to the negative bar, which is placed directly beneath the machines. From this negative bar a connection is run down into a cable pit, and the incoming negative cables are brought here through ducts laid in the floor. Provision has been made for eight incoming high tension cables, and the bus bar is broken up into sections by sectionalizing switches between adjacent sets of feeder and machine switches.

The oil switches are all 300 ampere General Electric Type "F," Form H-3, except the tie switch, which is 500 amperes capacity.

Two storage batteries are placed in the basement, each consisting of fifty-six $7\frac{3}{4}$ inch by $7\frac{3}{4}$ inch storage batteries; the normal discharge capacity being 15 amperes for 8 hours. These cells are Type "E," seven plate chloride accumulators. A 2 kilowatt electro-dynamic motor generator is provided for charging the batteries.

The switchboard for the control of all of the rotaries, together with the control of the cable and rotary oil switches, is on the operating floor. The alternating current instruments and switches are on the ends, with the heavy direct current machine panels next, and in the centre a rotary starting panel. This panel is equipped with a duplicate starting apparatus, with provision for starting the rotary converters either from the bus bars or from the induction motor generator provided for that purpose. This motor generator is a Westinghouse 650 to 550 volt shunt wound generator, direct connected to a 150 horse-power 3 phase 380 volt 25 cycle induction motor, having three 60 kilowatt 13,200 to 380 volt transformers.

The upper deck of the switchboard contains all the outgoing feeder panels. Each feeder panel has a capacity of 2000 amperes, and is arranged to take two cables of normal capacity of 1000 amperes. The entire switchboard is built of pink Tennessee marble, and all bus bars are of aluminium.

The West Philadelphia Substation (Substation No. 21), faces on Market Street, running parallel with Allison Street. The front elevation is very attractive, constructed of brick with a terra cotta cornice, with a central doorway 16 feet wide. The operating floor is 4 feet above the level of the pavement. By the doorway there is a recess the width of the door, 10 feet long and 4 feet deep, permitting of a wagon being backed into the building, so that any heavy machinery can be lifted by the crane and deposited in its proper position.

This is a 3 motor crane of 25 tons capacity and 36 feet span. The crane runway is of reinforced concrete supported on one side by pilasters built in the wall, and on the other side by brick piers, which also support the two sections of the roof.

The roof over the main portion of the building has a span of 38 feet, and is built of reinforced concrete with a slag covering. The roof over the oil switch and bus bar compartments is also built of reinforced concrete with a slag top, and has a span of 15 feet.

There are at present installed three 1500 kilowatt 600 volt Westinghouse rotary converters, but provision is made for three more units of the same capacity. The rotaries each receive their power from three 550 kilowatt 13,200 volt to 380 volt Westinghouse air blast transformers.

The high tension bus bar compartment is built of brick, with the disconnecting switches on one side and the oil switch compartments on the other. Between each set of cable and converter oil switches the bus bar is divided into sections connected by sectionalizing switches. Over the oil switches is a 1-ton Yale & Towne Triplex trolley block on single "I" beam crane.

High tension cables enter the building through ducts on the basement floor, and rise into compartments built in the operating floor. In these compartments are placed the cable current transformers. The cables then connect to the cable oil switch, passing under the high tension bus bar to the cable disconnecting switches, and then through heavy porcelain insulators to the three high tension bus bars.

The machine disconnecting switches connect to the high tension bus bars on the side opposite to the cable disconnecting switches. From the disconnecting switches the machine cables pass under the bus bar compartment to the machine oil switch, and thence to the machine current transformers, and to the main transformers over the air duct. The machine current transformers are in ducts built in the floor, and covered with slate slabs the same as the cable current transformers, except that they are on the opposite side of the high tension bus bar.

Under the transformers is the air duct, which has a cross-section of 110 square feet.

The oil switches are motor operated, of the General Electric Type "F," Form H-3, remote control, triple pole, single throw, capacity 300 amperes per phase. The power for operating these switches is furnished by 56 Type "E" seven plate chloride accumulator cells; size of plate $7\frac{3}{4}$ inches by $7\frac{1}{4}$ inches; normal discharge for 8 hours, 15 amperes.

The negative side of all the lighting in the building is brought to a number of 3-way switches. The normal position of these switches connects the lights to the ground. The other position connects the negative side of the lights to the positive of the battery, and the amount of charging current can be varied at the will of the operator by connecting as many circuits as desired to the battery.

In the basement, under the bus bar compartment, are installed two 90 inch American blower fans driven by $17\frac{1}{2}$ horse-power Westinghouse induction motors. These fans each have a capacity of 20,000 cubic feet of air (at one ounce pressure) per minute.

The wiring to the rotary converters is so arranged that any of the rotaries may be started from the direct current bus bar or by the motor generator installed for this purpose. The generator is 100 kilowatt, shunt wound, 650 to 550 volts, and is direct connected to a

150 horse-power 380 volt 3 phase induction motor. The induction motor is connected to three 60 kilowatt 13,200 to 380 volt air blast transformers through an auto starter.

The switchboard is 59 feet 2 inches long, and is built of pink Tennessee marble, set on a marble base. The alternating current instruments, together with the oil switch controlling switches, are on the end furthest from the door. The machine panels are in the middle of the board, and have a 4000 ampere Cutter overload and reverse current breaker on the top slab of each panel. On the middle slab is a 5000 ampere Weston Type "B" ammeter, placed alongside a General Electric 3000 ampere high capacity wattmeter. Below the wattmeter is placed the field switch. The bottom slab holds the contact arm and studs of the field rheostat, and the direct current rotary starting switch. The other end of the switchboard is made up of sixteen 2000 ampere feeder panels. Each panel is arranged to take two cables of 1000 amperes at normal rated capacity. The switches have a normal rating of 2000 amperes, and are the Anderson quick break type. All instrument and switch lugs are finished smooth and connected to the bus bars by special clamp lugs. The bus bars on this board are all made of aluminium.

R. B. SELFRIDGE
Secretary and Treasurer Philadelphia Rapid Transit Company

CONSTRUCTION OF THE SUBWAY

THE Philadelphia Subway occupies the bed of Market Street, from the Delaware River on the east to the Schuylkill River on the west, passing around City Hall by a loop in the bed of Juniper Street, Filbert Street, and West and South Penn Square.

East of Fifteenth Street the two local tracks are carried around the City Hall below the main Subway tracks, terminating in a substation at Juniper Street. The east Market Street section of the Subway contains two tracks.

West of Fifteenth Street there are four tracks. Two of these are a continuation of the tracks in the east Market Street section, connecting with the West Philadelphia Elevated to Sixty-ninth Street. The other two are for the local cars that run west from Juniper Street, cross the Schuylkill at grade, and continue on the surface tracks on Woodland and Lancaster Avenues.

Just east of Front Street, the Subway turns north to Arch Street, running thence to the terminal at Delaware Avenue and South Street on an elevated structure.

Interest in the Subway centres largely in this eastern section, built for the Philadelphia Rapid Transit Company by the Millard Construction Company. Its engineering problems are unique. It underlies a mile and more of the busiest street of the city. The route is lined on both sides with large buildings, many of them converted and added to from time to time, on old foundations that were a constant challenge to engineering skill. The street was riddled with a century's accumulation of gas and water pipes, sewers, electric conduits, and fire mains, in places too close together to admit a hand between them. They seriously hampered the excavating and the proper placing of structural material.

The problem before the Millard Company's engineers was that of building a double track Subway and of reconstructing the sewer system, building an adequate concrete sewer on each side behind the walls of the train tube; and also the rebuilding and rearranging of the telephone, telegraph, electric power and light, gas, water, and high pressure fire systems without interrupting the service in any of them.

The east Market Street section of the Subway is 5,888 feet long from Thirteenth Street to the portal. Its general width, out to out of walls, is about 37 feet, and the clear head room is 14 feet. The distance, centre to centre of tracks, is 13 feet 3 inches.

The Subway is a rectangular tunnel of reinforced concrete. The floor is flat, with steel supports for the ties embedded in the concrete. The structural thickness of the walls is 16 inches, disregarding minor variations. The roof is a flat slab resting on the side walls and on the central columns.

Drainage is provided under the whole length of the west-bound track. Inlets with grated covers are sunk every 50 feet in the centre of both tracks, those on the east-bound track being cross-connected to the main drain. The whole flow from the east Market Street section is collected in a well at Fifth Street, whence it is discharged into the north sewer by electric pumps.

All of the structural steel used in the Subway is covered with concrete, which protects the steel. The only iron visible is at the stations. A cast iron fender is provided for the foot of each column on the station platform, to protect it against the wear of the feet.

The eastern section has five stations—at Second, Fifth, Eighth, Eleventh and Thirteenth Streets. Ample entrances and exits are had through openings in the street and through passages to the chief department stores.

The two tracks are separated by a wall from the portal to Letitia Street, and westward of that point by a line of columns, which practically subdivides the Subway into two longitudinal compartments. Four places occur on the line where the roof has been built in a single span, the centre columns having been omitted. At these points are to be placed crossovers from one track to the other.

Station platforms are 350 feet long—long enough for a train of eight cars, should the conditions demand it. Near the edge of the platform anti-slipping strips of iron and carborundum are embedded in the concrete flush with the floor.

The stations at Eighth and Eleventh Streets are provided with overpassages, or bridges, giving access to both the east-bound and west-bound platforms from either side of the street.

The station at Thirteenth Street has an underpassage, leading from the local platform level of the City Hall section to both the east-bound and west-bound platforms of the East Market Street section.

All the stairways in the Subway are of reinforced concrete, with anti-slipping strips let into the treads.

The width of the stations is variable. Those at Eighth and Eleventh Streets are 100 feet wide, occupying generally the entire width between the house lines of Market Street. At Fifth Street the sewers on either side of the street occupy the space between foundation walls of the houses and the back of the station walls, and at Second Street the general width of the station is somewhat less than the width of the street.

The sewers follow generally lines distant 25 feet from the centre of Market Street on each side of the Subway. They either pass below the station platforms, as at Second Street, Eighth Street, Eleventh Street and Thirteenth Street; or are deflected, as at Fifth

WILLIAM S. TWINING
Chief Engineer Philadelphia Rapid Transit Company

Street, so as to pass between the foundation walls on each side of the street and the outside of the station walls. Both sewers vary in shape and cross-section. They are 7 feet by 7 feet at Front Street, and gradually reduce toward the western end of the drainage area, the north side sewer terminating in a section of rectangular shape, 4 feet by 3 feet 6½ inches, and the south side sewer terminating in a junction chamber, which gathers the flow from City Hall and South Juniper Street. At Sixth Street on the south sewer, a junction chamber is built to receive a future low level sewer.

Intercepting chambers are built in both the main sewers at Letitia Street. A cast iron pipe sewer, running at right angles to the main sewers, connects these sewers with each other and with a 3 foot diameter sewer that parallels the north sewer to a point near Delaware Avenue, where it joins a sewer which discharges at the pier head line in the Delaware River.

The Subway structure in general is built of reinforced concrete, and the stations of reinforced concrete and structural steel. The sewers are built of reinforced concrete, except where cast iron pipe has been substituted in a few places.

The material penetrated has been principally sand, gravel, and clay, with occasional pockets of running sand, and with comparatively little water.

The specifications provided that the entire work of construction should be done under cover of a wooden deck, to be placed at the level of the original surface of the street, so as to disturb traffic as little as possible, and not to cut off ingress and egress to the properties abutting on the work. The quickest method was found to be to excavate to a depth of 16 feet below the surface in open cut, after which the cut was decked over, and the material removed from below this depth through hatch holes, either previously prepared or cut in the deck as needed. The width of the trench varied, but the length of the cut operated on at one time was about 32 feet, for convenience of handling.

Prior to beginning the work, and also during the early stages, various methods of excavating were considered. It early became apparent that only the most primitive methods were possible, and the pick and shovel was adopted. The timbering, which was a necessary part of the work, as well as the underground structures, prevented the use of the ordinary excavating machinery.

The excavated earth was shovelled into one-half yard dumping buckets and hoisted to the surface, where it was loaded into wagons for removal to the dumps.

A stiff leg derrick, with a 35 foot boom, having a bull wheel and mounted on a movable carriage, with a house enclosing the operating machinery, was used. The maximum capacity of the machine was about 125 cubic yards per 10 hours; but this was reduced one-half on the average by the hindrance of the underground structures. The machinery consisted of a double drum hoist, with an independent swinging gear provided with foot power and electric brakes, and operated by a 25 horse-power motor. Direct current was used at 550 volts.

The total excavation was in the neighborhood of 400,000 cubic yards, or about 25,000 cubic yards to each machine.

Owing to different underground conditions, different methods of timbering had to be used from block to block. Sometimes the same method was not used throughout the entire length of one block. The entire work comes under the head of one or other of the following systems:

1st. Building each of the sewers separately, and then the entire cross-section of the Subway at one operation.

2d. Building the Subway wall and sewer on one side of the street, and the sewer only on the other; the remaining wall and roof of the Subway in a subsequent operation.

3d. Building both the Subway wall and sewer on each side of the street; the roof in a subsequent operation.

The second system was used on by far the largest portion of the standard Subway

The timbering at the stations as a rule required special handling, so as to clear not only the underground structures, but also the structural steel work as far as possible.

All of the timber used for shoring and bracing, excepting that for stringers under the rails, was short-leaf Virginia and North Carolina pine.

Systems of timbering are usually designed to follow what is known as "good practice," rather than to accord with the theories of earth pressure. The sizes of the timbers were adapted to the material of the excavation, and also the weight of the buildings on the banks, as well as to the width and depth of the ditch. They were first determined theoretically for certain assumed conditions, and afterwards so modified as to accord with best practice in this line of work.

The upper two sets of timbers were usually made considerably heavier than would be required by the pressures. On the upper set was laid the deck, and additional width had to be provided for breaking joints in the planking. On the second set was usually supported all of the underground structures, such as water and gas pipes, electric conduits, etc. Both of these sets were made solid; the braces were either in one piece or spliced to make them act as one piece. All of the other sets below the level of the second were provided with what are locally known as "false rangers." By means of this system it is possible to lift out a short length of brace to allow the construction to proceed without cutting out a brace reaching from side to side of the ditch, thereby preserving the integrity of the timbering as a whole. Each of the cross braces was secured in place with wooden wedges, driven from both sides simultaneously, following a timber which had been previously screw-jacked into place, to maintain the distance between the rangers.

Market Street Elevated Railway
Looking West toward Sixty-sixth Street Station

Four Steps in Track-laying, East Market Street Subway

GEORGE H. EARLE, JR.
Director Philadelphia Rapid Transit Company

The cross braces were generally placed 8 feet apart along the longitudinal axis of the Subway, and about 5 feet apart vertically. The distances between the timbers in both planes were frequently changed to clear obstructions as they were encountered.

Where both walls of the Subway were built before the core was removed from between them, the distance between the braces on the longitudinal axis of the Subway was about 12 feet. This distance could possibly have been increased to some extent had not the refill been made back of the Subway walls on both sides; the material was frequently piled up a considerable distance above the top of the walls and sloped back, forming practically two surcharged walls.

Of interest among the special cases mentioned, is that of supporting the banks at Front Street, above Market Street, where the Subway leaves the bed of Market Street. The excavation was made in the usual way, excepting that it was all open cut, and the banks were sustained by raker braces, placed as the excavation proceeded. The maximum cut was about 30 feet; the banks were heavy, and 60 feet from the front face of the cut were some quite heavy buildings. In the bed of Front Street was a sewer, with gas and water distribution pipes and electrical conduits, among which were the long distance telephone and others of equal importance, all of which were kept in undisturbed service throughout the entire work. The removal of the raker braces, as the work was built up under them, was quite a delicate matter, and had to be preceded in every case by the placing of others, so as not to disturb the banks.

At the street intersections, for expeditious working, the length of the trench was reduced, and generally the depth excavated in open cut was about 8 feet, after which it was decked over, and the balance of the excavated material removed under the deck.

Considerable advantage was gained by working the derricks in pairs, a derrick taking out the top lift being followed closely by another taking out all the material below that level.

All of the excavation along the sides was made in the above manner; but when the core was to be removed, a different method had to be adopted. The core was attacked from one side of the street by driving a heading or drift into the bank, and then the heading was enlarged by working both ways from it. The headings were usually about 8 feet in depth, which depth was maintained when the cut was lengthened. The excavation was then continued in a vertical plane in lifts of from 4 to 6 feet, until sub-grade was reached.

Before the side trenches were excavated, the granite block paving was removed. The street was opened alongside of and between the rails, and 12 inch by 14 inch stringers of long-leaf yellow pine were inserted under each rail below the ties. The spaces between the ties were then filled solid with planking; a layer of 2 inch plank was spiked on the ties parallel with the rails, and the granite block paving was replaced on a bed of sand.

After the side walls were built, before removing whatever timbers might have been in the way of the roof, it was necessary to place the needles to carry the two surface tracks across the excavation. Posts 8 inches by 10 inches were erected on the side walls at the level of the base of the arch, and two 12 inch by 12 inch 16 foot timbers were thrown across the excavation, resting on these posts and on a corbel set over a small post on each of the centre columns, at an elevation above the top of the roof. These needle beams were lashed together with 3 inch by 10 inch planks to prevent lateral movement, the weight of the street being depended on to hold them down.

Several variations of this method were used where necessary, as at the crossovers. Here the centre columns were omitted in the Subway structure, and the roof was put in in one span from wall to wall. At the crossovers west of Second Street Station, the finished roof was only a little below the street surface. The problem was to carry the street surface with its two lines of tracks across the Subway without a permanent intermediate support. The head-room below the street surface was insufficient for a truss to span the entire width of the structure, and the surface conditions did not allow of a bridge truss between the tracks, by which to suspend them from above.

An intermediate support was made of a small latticed steel column, supported about 1 inch above the finished underside of the roof slab on a 12 inch by 12 inch post resting on the Subway floor below. The needles were supported in the usual manner on this column, and on the posts erected on the side walls. The latticing on the column was arranged so as not to interfere with the reinforcing rods in either direction, and the column was concreted in the roof. In due time the wooden posts, which were set up on wedges, were lowered and then removed. The underside of the column, which had been raised above the forms, and which had been previously wrapped with close woven wire mesh, was plastered flush with the finished surface of the roof. This method worked so well, was so simple and comparatively inexpensive, that it was used on two other of the crossovers, although there was sufficient room above the roof for a truss to carry the street.

At another place, between Letitia Street and Front Street, where the Subway begins to rise to the surface, there was not sufficient room under the decking to conveniently place the concrete, the reinforcement, or the water-proofing. The rails were jacked up from the 12 inch by 14 inch stringers high enough to place 12 inch by 12 inch needles between the stringers and the rails. These needle beams were supported on the centre and side walls of the Subway on small lattice columns, as before, the stringers were removed, and the columns were concreted in the roof. The needles were placed 5 feet apart along the axis of the Subway, and the rails themselves carried the traffic over this span.

With several minor exceptions, all of the sheeting or sheet piling used on this work was of rough 2 inch by 8 inch planks, 12, 14, and 16 feet in length, and was hand driven.

At street intersections, and at the ends of side ditches, the bulkhead usually consisted of short lengths of sheeting, set in place as the excavation proceeded. This sheeting, which was in from 4 to 6 feet lengths, could not be driven, owing to the underground structures.

The decking consisted of two courses of planking—the upper course of 3 inch by 9 inch, laid close; the lower course of 4 inch by 10 inch, laid with 8 inch spaces between the planks. The lower course was laid parallel to the axis of the Subway, and spiked to the upper cross braces in the ditch with 80 penny wire spikes. The upper course was laid at right angles to the lower course. The decking supported all the wagon traffic on the street without any difficulty, and sustained unusually heavy concentrated loads at times.

The methods at the stations varied considerably from those in the Subway proper, as the stations occupied the entire width of the street, and the houses had to be underpinned.

At Second Street the station wall is about 9 feet from the house line, and the deepest excavation is at least 20 feet below the bottom of the average foundation. The buildings were all four and five story stores and light manufacturing buildings and warehouses, and were quite old, although none of them was extraordinarily heavy.

At Fifth Street the excavation occupies the entire width between the houses, and all of the houses were underpinned. The foundations were carried down to the level of the bottom of the new sewers, which abutted immediately against the houses. All of the buildings were old and some of them quite heavy.

At Eighth Street the excavation occupies the entire width between the houses, and nearly all the houses were underpinned. All the buildings, except those adjacent to the southeast quarter of the station, were very heavy, and were occupied by department stores.

At Eleventh Street the excavation occupies the entire width of the street, and all of the adjacent buildings were underpinned. Some of the buildings, as at the southeast corner of Eleventh Street, were exceedingly heavy and the foundations were anything but ideal, because the original was quite old, and had been added to from time to time.

The underpinning at the southwest corner of Eleventh Street was light, but at 1107 and 1109 Market Street was quite difficult. The latter buildings were exceedingly heavy, and the subsoil was a tenacious blue clay.

At Thirteenth Street the buildings adjacent to the northeast, northwest, and southeast quarters of the station were underpinned, but presented no unusual difficulties. The building at the southwest corner was founded at a lower level than any of the adjacent Subway work.

At quite a number of places, particularly where the Subway passes close to house foundations, underpinning was necessary to prevent settlement or undermining of the buildings.

Three distinct methods of underpinning were adopted, based on the character of the foundations. In every case the excavation was completed to the level of the bottom of the foundations before beginning the underpinning.

1st. Continuous underpinning without the aid of needles.
2d. Continuous underpinning using needle beams.
3d. Isolated pier underpinning using needle beams.

The first method was used where continuous foundations existed, and where the depth of the underpinning was not too great. The soil was removed from under the foundation walls in alternate sections, 6 to 8 feet in length, the sides of the excavation being sheeted progressively. Masonry, usually concrete, was built up to a point from 24 to 30 inches below the bottom of the original footings (or, where it was necessary to remove the original footing as being unsound, up to the level of the sound masonry). The space between the original work and the new work was filled with brick masonry in cement mortar, and the work was finally wedged up hard with steel wedges against the old masonry. Each section was completed before a new one was started, and the arch action of the masonry was depended on to carry the building temporarily while the section of underpinning was being completed.

This method was used at the northwest corner of Eighth and Market Streets with complete success, and without causing the slightest apparent settlement.

Considerable continuous underpinning with needle beams was done around Front Street. The underpinning was from 25 to 30 feet deep. The excavation was taken down to the bottom of the footing. Crib holes were sunk inside and outside of the buildings. These holes were short sheeted, as the excavation was carried down, in sections of about 4 feet. The crib holes outside the building were usually carried down to the depth of the proposed foundation. Cribs of 12 inch by 12 inch timbers were built up to a level above the bottom of the footings, usually sufficiently high to allow working space above the cellar floors for cutting out holes for the needles in the foundation walls. Unless the buildings were heavy, the inside cribs were not carried down more than about 4 feet below the cellar floors. These cribs were capped with heavy timbers, usually 12 inch by 12 inch and 12 inch by 14 inch, between which were placed the jack screws. The cribs inside and outside the buildings were usually about 20 feet, centre to centre. The requisite number of 20 inch steel "I" beams to carry the load, each about 24 feet long, were placed on the crib caps through holes in the foundation walls, and wedged up with steel wedges and with shingles, so as to take the weight of the buildings. After this the earth was excavated below the foundations, between the inside and outside crib holes. Short sheeting as above described was placed as the excavation proceeded. The cribs were braced against each other, and also against the banks as the excavation was removed.

CLARENCE WOLF
Director Philadelphia Rapid Transit Company

Signal Apparatus, West Market Street

Subway-Elevated Car
Three-Car Train at Thirty-second Street Station

In this kind of underpinning it is usual to place on top of the needle beams smaller "I" beams immediately under the walls, to carry the walls between the needles. These were discovered to be an unnecessary refinement, and were omitted in the greater part of the work. Their omission made it far easier for the brickmason to make the closure between the concrete in the new foundations and the old foundation walls, which were usually of rubble masonry.

Isolated underpinning with needle beams was used to a considerable extent. The cribs inside and outside the buildings were employed as usual. "I" beams, spanning from crib to crib, were usually made to carry a saddle, from which were suspended secondary "I" beams, which carried the pier footing. After the weight was taken by the jack screws, the excavation was made below the pier bottom for the underpinning. Where the piers were sufficiently large, they were sometimes pierced the same as solid walls, for the passage of the "I" beams resting on jack timbers on the cribs, and the work conducted as with continuous underpinning.

A good example of this character of work, where the pier was suspended, was at the southwest quarter of Eighth Street Station, where an iron front, nine stories in height, is carried on one column and the party walls of the adjoining buildings. Another example is the property 1109 Market Street, where two piers were underpinned by piercing the piers with needle beams, the load on each pier being in the neighborhood of 200,000 pounds.

The Market Street front of the properties stretching east from the northeast corner of Eighth Street, consisted of a number of piers with curtain walls between them. As these walls carry no load whatever, no special precaution was taken to protect them. The piers, however, were underpinned by a variation from the usual method with isolated piers. As it was found impracticable to build cribs inside the buildings, each individual pier was supported by means of what the underpinners call "spur braces" or spurs. These consist of a couple of raker braces placed against the pier to be underpinned, supported at the base on cribbing, and carrying at the top a head piece or cap, from which a sill is suspended by means of rods. On this sill piece, and in a seat provided between the raker braces, are supported several "I" beams, cantilevering under the pier foundation, which is undermined one section at a time and underpinned.

On Market Street west of Front Street, the Subway begins to curve into the private right-of-way of the Philadelphia Rapid Transit Company. The Subway passes directly under the house at the northwest corner of Front and Market Streets. The north wall enters on the house line of Market Street at the party line between the corner property and the house west of Front Street, and emerges on the west house line of Front Street on the party line between the corner property and the first house north of the corner property.

The whole west and south fronts of the building are, therefore, supported on the Subway roof. These two walls were needled in the usual way for continuous underpinning, the cribs and needles being so placed as to allow the building of the north and centre walls of the Subway in sections. When these sections were built, the weight of the needles was transferred to a series of "drums," as the underpinners call them—vertical posts set up on jack screws; the cribs were removed, and the several sections of Subway walls connected. Permanent steel girders were built in the Subway roof, for the purpose of carrying the future foundations of a heavy building to be erected at this point. The drums were arranged so as to allow the placing of these girders as far as possible without changing the temporary work. When these girders were in place the weight of the building was transferred to them, and all the temporary work was removed. The concrete roof of the Subway was then built between these girders, and the masonry underpinning of the buildings was completed on top of the Subway roof. Sixty-five buildings were underpinned on this work with frontages varying from 20 feet to 150 feet.

All of the concrete was mixed by machinery, in approximately one-half-yard batches. The revolving drum type of machine with loose paddles was used, and gave entire satisfaction. Since the machine could not be loaded with a derrick, because of insufficient room, some compact mechanical means had to be provided—a device moreover which could readily be dismantled and moved as the concrete mixer was moved along the line of the work. Two distinct types of elevating devices were developed, and, it is believed, first used on this work.

Each of the mixers was mounted on a carriage to facilitate handling from place to place, and each mixer was driven independently by a 10 horse-power electric motor mounted on the carriage.

Water was supplied the mixers from temporary connections made with the water distribution pipes on the street. The concrete was made of that consistency which required an amount of water equal to about 16 per cent. of the quantity of mortar.

Under the discharge end of the machine was placed a sheet iron lined wooden trough, with an iron lifting gate, the box of a capacity of a whole batch of mixed concrete.

The concrete was deposited in the work through chutes in the deck, discharging either into the forms or on to platforms provided for the purpose.

During the winter months each mixer outfit was augmented by a vertical steam boiler of 10 to 12 commercial horse-power, for the purpose of heating the water, sand and stone. A 2 inch pipe with cross arms of 1 inch pipe at right angles to it, pierced with $\frac{1}{8}$ inch holes, and connected with the boilers with a short length of steam hose, served to supply sufficient heat to prevent freezing by blowing live steam into the sand and stone. A permanent 1 inch connection was taken off the boilers and turned down into the water barrel, which was

W. H. CARPENTER
Director Philadelphia Rapid Transit Company

mounted on a platform back of the concrete machine, and served to heat the water used in mixing the concrete. No precautions were taken to prevent freezing of the concrete, other than covering it with salt hay after it had been placed, even when the temperature at the street surface was as low as 15° Fahrenheit. No bad effects of the freezing of the concrete are noticeable in the work constructed at low temperatures.

In addition to the seven $\frac{1}{2}$-yard mixers, there was provided a small portable Smith machine, driven by a gasoline engine, and mounted on a wagon body. This machine was an improvement over the larger machines of the same make, in that the drum was dumped by simply depressing a lever, instead of by operating a screw, which required considerably more time. This machine was a valuable adjunct, being used wherever the quantity of concrete to be placed would not warrant the use of the larger machine. It was easily demonstrated that this was really the proper type of concrete mixer for work that requires either constant and expensive shifting of mixing plant, or wheeling of concrete quite long distances, which was not advisable for several reasons outside of its cost. The machine was easily drawn by a pair of horses, and was ready for instant operation. It could be placed on the surface in such a position with relation to the work as either to pour the concrete directly into the forms below or greatly to reduce the length of wheel.

Three mixtures of concrete were used in the work: $1:2:4$; $1:2\frac{1}{2}:5$; and $1:3:6$. The $1:2:4$ concrete was used in all places where work was below the level of the permanent ground water, and in particularly thin sections. The $1:2\frac{1}{2}:5$ mixture was used in all work pertaining to the Subway proper; and the $1:3:6$ mixture was used in the sewers and sewerage appurtenances.

The material used in the aggregate was pebbles varying from $\frac{1}{8}$ inch to 1 inch diameter, dredged from the bed of the Delaware River near Bordentown, N. J., and completely washed in the process of screening. They were beautifully graded, and formed a far denser concrete than is ordinarily to be had with broken stone. This point is mentioned because this is probably the first large piece of work in this vicinity in which gravel was used for this purpose. The sand was principally a coarse gray sand, well graded and washed, dredged in the Delaware River opposite Gloucester, N. J., and is locally known as "Gloucester Beach" sand. Several brands of cement were used, but by far the major portion of the work was built with "Vulcanite" cement.

The capacity of the concrete plant provided was far in excess of the needs for the actual mixing; but experience showed that in placing the concrete the truest economy restricted the length of wheel to not over 150 feet. Furthermore, as the timber had to be changed as the work was built up, it was necessary, therefore, to suspend work temporarily at a given place from time to time. For this reason, if portable machines of sufficient capacity had been provided, which could readily have been moved from place to place, fewer of them would have been needed.

Each machine has mixed upwards of 12,000 cubic yards of concrete. The capacity of the individual mixing machines used on this work was determined by the rapidity with which the concrete could be placed; about 75 cubic yards in 10 hours is the maximum quantity handled by a mixer on this work.

The reinforcing rods were twisted steel of the Ransome pattern, supplied by the Carnegie Steel Company; 5,500,000 pounds were used. As many of these rods had to be bent to different radii, the question of a power machine for that purpose arose early in the work. No machine was available for bending twisted rods. Ordinary square or round bars could be bent on a tire bender, but not twisted rods.

A machine had to be devised for the purpose, taking into account the fact that the bars for the sewers had to be bent to varying radii, and to have a piece of tangent at both ends.

The general principle of the machine as built is that of the tire bender. Corrugated case hardened rolls were used in place of plain ones, as in the ordinary tire bender. The adjustable roll was actuated by a hand wheel operating a rack and pinion, which determined the position of the roll, and consequently the radius of curvature. By running this roll entirely out of the plane of the rods while the machine was in motion, the rods came out without being bent, thus providing the proper tangent section on the end of the rods. The machine was geared to operate rapidly, and was heavily built. It was driven by a link belt from a $4\frac{1}{2}$ horse-power electric motor. It bent any size of rod up to 1 inch square to any radius up to 9 feet. A graduated scale set on the rack indicated when the roll was in the proper position to bend any given radius.

The designing of forms for use on this work required that several distinct points be kept in view. They should be:

1st. Of as simple construction as possible, to allow of rapid dismantling or collapsing.

2d. As compact units as possible, to allow of handling under the street surface and in cramped positions generally.

3d. As strong as possible, to allow of constant re-using.

4th. As light as possible for facility of handling.

North Carolina pine, fairly free from sap, was used throughout, excepting in some instances where panelling was required, where white pine was used.

Both tongued and grooved and beveled edged stuff were used. The sheeting or lagging for the main walls and slab roof was 2 inch by 10 inch plank, generally 16 feet in length, tongued and grooved, and planed on both sides. The necessity of accurately centring the tongue and groove where plank are planed both sides is obvious.

MAYOR JOHN E. REYBURN
Director Philadelphia Rapid Transit Company

The following spacing of uprights was allowed with sheeting or lagging of different thicknesses:

Distance between Supports	Commercial Size of Sheeting or Lagging
48 inch centres	2 inches
36 " "	1½ "
30 " "	1 inch
18 " "	¾ "

In designing the forms the concrete was assumed to weigh 150 pounds per cubic foot, and the allowable unit stress in the timber used was taken at 1,000 pounds per square inch.

The forms used for encasing the centre line columns in concrete were made of 1¼ inch stuff, properly battened. Three sides of this form were made the entire length of the column and hinged together, and the other side was placed as the form was filled with concrete. The fourth side was made in sections about 3 feet long, each section being held in position with loose battens, which were supported in notched pieces set on and protruding beyond the adjacent sides. Wooden wedges were used between the loose battens and the sectional front boards of the form to hold them in position. The form itself was held in position in the following manner: The centre line columns were built of structural shapes, generally four angles, and several tie plates were arranged so that the web was transverse to the centre line of the Subway. The forms were set around the steel column on a previously built plinth or base of concrete, and were held at a distance of 1½ inches from the steel on all sides by 40 penny nails driven through the form on the line of the web of the column, to hold the form from moving in the direction of the longitudinal axis of the Subway. Motion in the other direction was prevented by nails driven through the side leaves of the form and just touching the steel angles. No other bracing of any kind was required. The forms were filled at one operation, being removed after 30 hours. The column caps were made of light lagging, each side being battened together and the four sides bolted, so as to admit of easy removal and re-erection.

Crude oil was used for greasing the forms to prevent adhesion of the concrete, and was found to be satisfactory.

The following rules were observed in removing roof forms, subject, of course, to variation due to the conditions of temperature and moisture, etc.:

Standard roof: Leave forms in at least 3 weeks;
  Load (street car tracks) can be put on in 5 weeks.

Crossover roof: Leave forms in at least 5 weeks;
  Load (street car tracks) can be put on in 7 weeks.

  Centre posts in crossover can be removed at any time after centres are removed.

Station roof: Leave forms in at least 1 week;
  Load (street car tracks) can be put on in 2 weeks.

If it became necessary to load the structure before the expiration of the required time, the forms were allowed to remain in place until that time had elapsed.

After placing the concrete roof, and while the needles were still in position, the water-proof layer was applied. The water-proofing consists of a sheet of asphaltic mastic, and was placed in two layers, each $\frac{1}{2}$ inch in thickness. The 8 inch by 10 inch posts which support the needles on the side walls and over the centre columns, were boxed around so that the lower layer of water-proofing should be kept away from the posts at least 2 inches on each side. The 3 inch layer of concrete intended as a protective coating for the water-proofing against physical injury, was then placed, and before the needles were removed the longitudinal stringers under the rails were posted on the main roof with 8 inch by 10 inch posts, set on 4 inch foot blocks about 5 feet centre to centre.

The needles were then withdrawn and the posts supporting the needles removed. The asphalt was patched out so as to form a continuous sheet, and the upper layer of concrete was completed.

At the stations, where the street was carried on the structural steel as soon as it was placed, the procedure was quite similar. The posts were boxed around as in the former case, the asphalt sheet laid on top of the concrete jack arches, and the 3 inch protective layer placed. The permanent posts were then placed, resting on the finished roof, and the temporary posts and boxing removed from on the steel girders. The lower layer of concrete was carried up over the steel to the level of the bottom of the water-proofing, after which the asphalt layer was patched out as usual, and the protective layer was completed.

After the boxing was removed so as to allow the placing of the lower layer of water-proofing, it was again restored prior to placing the upper layer at a distance of about 4 inches each side beyond the lower layer, so that the top layer will lap over the lower layer to form a continuous sheet.

At Second Street Station the sewers and all of the station work were completed and the structural steel erected on the sides before the removal of the core was begun. The top lift (about 8 feet in depth) was then taken out of the core, and the transverse steel girders were placed in position from each side. These girders eventually rested on the centre columns in the stations. They were posted down as each successive lift of the core was removed, until sub-grade was reached. The concrete centre footing was then built and the columns erected on them, and the cross girders riveted in place.

After the cross girders were placed in the top lift the entire street load was carried on them during the work of excavation. The girders were spaced 6 feet centre to centre, and were temporarily bolted to the longitudinal girders at the sides, the other ends being supported on 12 inch by 12 inch timbers, 18 feet long, placed in two lines parallel with the axis of the Subway, and about 5 feet from centre to centre. The needles, as they were known in the work, were posted down to the bottom.

No timbering other than the needles above mentioned and the posts supporting them, was required in the core. The posts were 12 inch by 12 inch timbers, 16 feet long, at subgrade of the excavation. They were tied together transversely and along the axis of the Subway with 3 inch by 8 inch planks, to prevent distortion or movement.

Practically the same method of erection was followed at Fifth, Eighth, and Eleventh Street Stations. At Thirteenth Street Station the entire cut was timbered, and the steel placed afterwards.

All of the structural steel at the stations was placed with one or other of the derricks described above. A portable "A" frame was used for lowering the centre Subway columns, and a gin pole and portable winch were used in placing the steel work at the portal, which was not accessible to a derrick.

The erection of the structural steel often presented great difficulties. Since the material could not always be lowered into the places where it was required on account of the underground structures, it had to be put in wherever there was an opening in the structures, and then skidded along underneath to its proper place.

The steel work was riveted with pneumatic hammers supplied with air by portable electric driven air compressors.

The building of the sewers generally required four distinct operations: 1st, The laying of the concrete invert; 2d, the placing of the brick lining in the invert; 3d, the building of the two side walls to the spring line of the arch; 4th, the placing of the arch.

Wooden templets were used for forming up the invert, and wooden side forms were generally used below the springing line of the arch; collapsible steel forms were used for the arch in every case. The outside forms for the arch were generally built up as the concrete was placed, of 1 inch by 6 inch rough lagging, on ribs cut from 1 inch boards 12 inches wide, and spaced 30 inches centre to centre.

Two sets of transverse reinforcing bars were used in the arch and side walls; one set was usually placed 2 inches above the intrados of the arch, and the other 2 inches below the extrados. These rods were set after the forms for the side walls were built to the spring line. They were supported on the centre line of the arch at the proper height on 2 inch by 3 inch scantlings, suspended from the trench timbers in notches cut so as to preserve the proper distance centre to centre, and by 1 inch by 3 inch planks fastened to the top of the side forms at the spring line of the arch.

The longitudinal rods were wired to the transverse rods in the proper position.

The collapsible steel arch forms were set on sills parallel to the axis of the sewer, framed together so as to form a carriage which was provided with cast iron wheels or casters. The entire section of the arch after lowering the crown could be moved on wooden rails supported above the invert, which were provided for the purpose.

The equivalent of 50 feet of completed sewer, 7 feet by 7 feet in dimension, is the maximum length built in this manner in one day of 10 hours.

It was early recognized that the one thing that stood in the way of rapid progress in the construction of the Subway, was the maintenance of the old Market Street sewer until such time as the new sewers could be put into operation. As long as the old sewer in the centre of the street remained in service, it was impossible to excavate for the Subway proper. The only work that could be done on the Subway, throughout its whole length, was the building of the side walls.

Several schemes for getting rid of the obstruction were considered. It was proposed to begin operations on the new sewers on both sides of the street simultaneously, block by block; to connect up the house services and inlets as the sewers were completed; and also to make temporary connection with the old sewer to the westward where necessary. It was also proposed to establish small pumping plants along the line to pump the sewage and storm water from the several disconnected sections of the new sewers into the higher level sewers on the intersecting streets at Fourth, Seventh, Ninth, Twelfth Streets, etc.

By dividing the new sewers into comparatively small sections the quantity to be pumped at each point could be minimized.

Work on the Subway proper could then have been commenced at several points at the same time without waiting for the completion of any considerable length of new sewer or even before the outlet of the new sewers was completed.

This scheme was considered in all its details, and the necessary computations were made. It was found that if an amount of storm water due to a rainfall on the drainage area at the rate of 3 inches per hour for a period of twenty minutes was deemed sufficient, the tributary sewers were all sufficiently large to accommodate the increased flow. Under ordinary circumstances this would have presented a splendid solution of the problem, and would no doubt have hastened the completion of the whole work. But the uncertainty of being able to put the several pumping plants into instant operation during a storm was allowed to outweigh the good points of the plan, in view of the incalculable damage that might have ensued.

The only other feasible method was the construction of the Subway, following the building of the new sewers from the outlet continuously, and this method was, therefore, adopted.

As can well be imagined, the underground structures seriously interfered with the work. In some places, particularly at the street intersections where two distinct sets of structures were encountered, they were often in such a number, and were so close together, and of

AUGUST B. LOEB
Director Philadelphia Rapid Transit Company

Construction of Concrete Floor, Market Street Elevated Railway
Sewer Construction, East Market Street Subway

Delaware Avenue Elevated Railway
Schuylkill River Bridge

such size, as to entirely preclude the idea of working a bucket between them, and the excavated material had to be removed by tunneling.

The material below the structures was either cast or wheeled to a point from which it could be taken to the surface in buckets in the usual manner. Often the space occupied by a duct manhole near a street intersection was used for the purpose of a shaft, the cables in the manhole being first drawn to one side and boxed in and the manhole demolished.

Some conduits, notably those made up of creosoted wood ducts, commonly called pump logs, could be moved aside without injury; but others, such as the wrought iron pipes carrying light and power cables, were inflexible and had to be maintained in position. Terra cotta ducts, enveloped in concrete casings, were likewise immovable, and had to be supported in the timbering in practically the same position they occupied in the ground. All of the structures, conduits and pipes were either blocked up from the trench timbering or suspended by wire cables or wooden hangers.

The high pressure fire service pipe, in addition to being blocked up from the timber, was firmly held in place by four 3 inch by 9 inch struts, abutting against the pipe so as to prevent any movement whatever.

The old abandoned wooden water pipes and several lines of abandoned conduits were removed as they were encountered. The two lines of 6 inch cast iron water pipes, which had been in service about 76 years, were replaced by 10 inch lines on each side of the street.

The 20 inch water distribution pipe, which is a modern structure, was relaid in the centre of the street, to allow the laying of a new line of ducts for the Keystone Telephone Company, whose old conduit was in the way of the Subway and sewers.

The Market Street sewer system which had to be replaced, had not been built at any one operation, but had been extended from time to time. Much of it had been built before the consolidation of the townships, districts and boroughs, which subsequently became the City of Philadelphia.

It was apparent that very little attention had been given to the grade of the invert, and none whatever to the hydraulic grade line due to a storm covering the drainage basin coincident with high tide in the river.

The sewer, excepting a small section built in 1898, was found to be in a badly dilapidated condition, and was often considerably distorted; the sewer invert in many cases appeared to be laid without the use of any cementing material of any kind.

Owing to abrupt grade changes and to defective junctions with intersecting sewers, a considerable part of the sewer cross-section (at times as much as 50 per cent.) was found to be obstructed with inorganic sediment which had been deposited during many years.

These defects, together with its fundamental defect of being too small to accommodate the flow, caused backing up during excessive storm—a condition indicated in the specifications for the sewers, by a clause which pointed out that the sewers at times "worked under a head." It was necessary, therefore, to provide for sealing house services and other connections against back flow.

The only successful method discovered was the relaying of the entire connection with a temporary one of light weight cast iron soil pipe with leaded joints, across the excavation. This method was subsequently adopted on the entire work.

As the new sewers were completed the house drainage was turned into them, as well as the flow from the old sewer. But it was impossible to build the new sewers continuously because of obstructions. The flow was, therefore, turned into the north and south sewers alternately as the gaps were closed up, and the sewers became continuous to the river.

The temporary connections between the old and the new sewers were made at the following places:

West of Fourth Street, into the north sewer;
East of Eighth Street, into the south sewer;
East of Tenth Street, into the north sewer;
At Eleventh Street, into the south sewer;
At Twelfth Street, into the south sewer;
At Thirteenth Street, into the north sewer.

Because of a gap in the south sewer west of Eighth Street, which could not be closed at the time, the entire sewage flow between Eighth and Thirteenth Streets on the south side was pumped across the street into the north sewer, which had been completed to that point for a period of over six months.

Two 4 inch electrically driven centrifugal pumps were used for this purpose. One pump was of ample capacity to handle the flow, and the other was provided as a reserve.

The working capacity provided by the new sewers is about four times that of the old when the latter was clean and unobstructed.

Among the pipes which were found in service were the two 6 inch lines of cast iron bell and spigot water pipe laid on each side of the street in 1822. These are among the first cast iron water pipes laid in the city. They were imported from England, no cast iron water pipe being made in this country at the time.

This pipe was cast in 9 foot lengths, and the bells were somewhat deeper than those of the present day. It was cast in a horizontal position, resulting in a thickness varying from $\frac{1}{4}$ inch to $\frac{3}{4}$ inch. When uncovered and no longer supported by the earth, it was ready to go to pieces on the slightest provocation; in many cases without any provocation at all. It was possible to drive a nail into the best of it with very little exertion.

On both sides of the street the excavation brought to light the old wooden water pipes which were laid in the year 1799 and first used in 1801. These pipes were simply hemlock logs, with a 6 inch hole bored through them. They were laid in continuous lengths, the end of one pipe being cut so as to fit into the adjacent one. Water was pumped at Centre Square Water Works, now the site of the City Hall. The wood was in most cases discovered to be sound.

Among the conduits encountered was that of the National Underground Electric Company, laid in 1883-84 from Second Street to City Hall. This is said to be the first electrical conduit laid in the City of Philadelphia. It consisted of about twenty 2 inch tin tubes or pipes embedded in a bituminous composition. There were also found the iron pipe conduits of the Brooks Underground Electric Company, which when in service were filled with paraffine or some similar substance, to provide insulation for the wires.

One of the conditions imposed was the relaying of the whole length of the Market Street high pressure fire main, with its many and intricate cross connections. The old 16 inch line was dismantled in sections only after the new one was laid and ready to connect up, since not more than one fire hydrant at a time might be put out of service.

Both the old and the new lines were temporarily supported in the timbering. Despite the fact that the line is at all times under a pressure of 50 pounds per square inch, when not in service, and in time of fire under a pressure of from 250 to 300 pounds, the service was never interfered with. The new line and all the hydrant connections were tested at 400 pounds per square inch prior to putting into service. The line, as long as it was supported in the timbering, was patrolled night and day for the purpose of observing its condition.

Since there is no circulation in the line when not in actual fire service, it was thought expedient to protect it against freezing. The entire pipe line and all its connections were wrapped with two 1 inch layers of hair felt, wired on and covered on the outside with tar paper to protect the felt from the rain or melting snow. The edges of the tar paper were lapped at least 6 inches, and hot tar was applied to the joints to make the covering continuous.

This same system of insulation was applied to all the water distribution pipes and house services, excepting the 20 inch distribution line, the circulation in which was sufficient to prevent freezing.

The Bell Telephone conduits, which occupied a position on the south side of the street, varied in dimension at different points. The average size was not far from four feet square. This conduit seems to have been an experimental one, and was composed of several quite distinct types of ducts. A portion of the line was fibre duct, another of creosoted wood duct, another of terra cotta duct, and still another of wrought iron pipe with screw joints. All of these ducts, excepting the wooden ones, were encased in concrete, which had to be stripped off before this conduit could be shifted or raised. This was a tedious operation, which had to be done without interfering with the service. The ducts not occupied by telephone cables were removed. It was often necessary either to shift the old ducts aside or to jack them up. Each individual duct was suspended from the upper cross brace with wire during the process of laying the new line. The new Bell Telephone conduit is built of terra cotta multiple duct (6-way) encased in concrete. In many places it occupies practically the same location in the street as did the original.

Owing to the obstructions encountered and to the incidental work it is difficult to make a direct comparison between this work and that built elsewhere in this country. But the fact remains that the construction of nearly 6,000 feet of Subway, with five stations, and of nearly 13,000 feet of sewers, and the rearrangement and rebuilding of the entire system of underground structures, as well as the underpinning of the buildings, and various other work incident to the construction, in the short time of two years, is an accomplishment which compares very favorably with the best in the construction of similar works.

The maximum number of men employed, by classes, was as follows:

Excavation, about	1000
Timbermen, about	160
Carpenters, about	125
Concrete, about	300
Structural steel erectors, about	95
Engineers, motor runners and pumpmen, about	40
Machinists, blacksmiths, pipe fitters, etc., about	30
Electricians, riggers, watchmen, about	35
Underpinners, about	50
Drivers, about	200
Double teams employed, about	200

The quantities of the principal items of construction used are as follows:

Excavation	398,661 cubic yards
Concrete	64,000 cubic yards
Brick masonry	2,000 cubic yards
Underpinning	2,122 cubic yards
Electric cable ducts	1,275,000 duct feet
Cast iron	200 tons
Structural steel	3,605 tons
Reinforcing rods for concrete	2,650 tons
Terra cotta pipe	10,050 lineal feet
Reinforced concrete sewers, from 3 ft. diam. to 7 ft. x 7 ft.	11,585 lineal feet
Vault lights	23,000 square feet

Manhole in Subway
Switchboard Wiring Conduits, Delaware Ave. Power Plant
High and Low Tension Cables, Sansom St. Substation
Ash Hoist, Delaware Avenue Power Plant

Subway Platform, Showing Cross-over from Platform to Platform
Subway Platform, Showing Ticket Booth

J. J. SULLIVAN
Director Philadelphia Rapid Transit Company

SCHUYLKILL RIVER BRIDGE AND ELEVATED RAILWAY STRUCTURES

THE Schuylkill River Bridge was commenced on July 6, 1903, and was completed in August, 1905. It is the twentieth bridge constructed over the Schuylkill River within the city limits, ten of which are for streets, and ten for railways.

The structure is 576 feet long and carries four tracks, two for the elevated railway trains, which operate on the elevated structure, and thence pass to the Subway east of the river, and two for the street railway cars which converge from the surface lines in West Philadelphia into the Subway.

It was decided to bridge the river, as the cost of tunnelling and the difficulty in providing space for an incline from a tunnel to the elevated structure was practically prohibitory. After an examination of the Market Street city bridge, with a view to altering and reinforcing it to carry the elevated railway, it was decided to build a new bridge with its centre line 100 feet north of the centre line of the city bridge. The approaches on each side of the river were planned to be built within the new limits of Market Street as widened on the north by ordinance of Councils passed in 1902. Space was thus provided for the curves connecting the bridge with the Subway and the Elevated. The elevation of the bridge, and consequently the grade on the eastern approach incline, was determined by the overhead clearance needed at the tracks of the railroad on the east bank of the Schuylkill. This was made 17 feet 4 inches, equal to other overhead clearances in the vicinity on this railroad. The clearance line over the channel is 26 feet $4\frac{1}{2}$ inches above mean high water.

The two outside tracks on the structure are used for the street cars and are about at the level of the surface of Market Street. The two inner tracks carry the elevated railway trains, which ascend to the west on an inclined floor on a 4.32 per cent. grade to meet the elevated structure.

The east and west channel piers and the west shore piers were founded by timber caissons sunk by the pneumatic method to bed rock and filled with concrete. The east shore pier was built in open coffer-dam and founded on bed rock. The depth of the rock at the various piers is as follows:

> East shore pier 16 feet below ground.
> East river pier 16 feet below mean high water.
> West river pier 39 feet below mean high water.
> West shore pier 37 feet below mean high water.

The foundation for the west shore pier comprised two caissons united by an arch. Some interference was encountered with the original coffer-dam for the "Permanent Bridge" over the Schuylkill River on the line of Market Street. This bridge was finished in 1804. It was noteworthy in its day, and was indeed a remarkable achievement without modern appliances.

The caissons were successfully founded without special difficulty and gave positive control of the bottoms upon which the foundations were built, since they were thoroughly inspected and tested before concreting. Concrete of the following mixture was used: 100 pounds of Portland cement; 3 cubic feet of fine gravel, or coarse sand; 5 cubic feet of crushed stone. On the east river pier, where some of the concrete was deposited in water, the concrete was lowered in buckets with trap doors at the bottom to discharge as closely as possible to the desired location, and to prevent wash.

The piers above the caisson foundations are built of a hard sandstone quarried at Lumberville on the Delaware River. The coping and the bridge seats are of granite. In this work is also included the reconstruction of part of the 25 foot retaining wall west of the Pennsylvania Railroad tracks on the west bank of the river. This was remodeled to serve as an abutment for the west span and the first columns of the elevated railway. As the retaining wall was built on piles part of it over the site of the abutment had to be torn down and remodeled to equalize the load of the bridge structure and the pressure of the 25 feet of earth behind the wall.

The foundations for the west legs of the tower at the eastern end of the elevated railway and immediately west of the abutment on the filling back of the retaining wall was also included in the work. Steel cylinders 4 feet in diameter were sunk to good gravel bottom below the original natural surface, the lower portion of the sinking being accomplished by the pneumatic process. The cylinders were filled with concrete. To keep the cylinders in their proper position relative to the abutment and to avoid injurious secondary stress in the tower above, the cylinders were connected to the abutment by struts embedded in concrete.

The superstructure comprises five spans, three of riveted lattice and two of plate girder construction. The riveted spans include the main channel span in the centre, which is 214.59 feet long, centre to centre of piers; and the adjoining spans on the east (98.27 feet) and west (90.05 feet). The span at each end is a plate girder, connecting the bridge with the Subway on the east and the Elevated on the west.

Each of the lattice spans has four trusses, with the inclined tracks for the elevated railway trains between the two inner trusses, and with the tracks for the street cars immediately within the outer trusses and approximately on the level of Market Street. A sidewalk 6 feet 6 inches wide is built on brackets outside of the north truss. While all four tracks are at about the same level at the eastern end, at the west end the train tracks are 23.8 feet above those for the street cars, so that the west plate girder span is a double decked structure.

The bridge was designed for a live load consisting of elevated trains with 25,000 pounds on each axle and of surface cars with 12,000 pounds on each axle.

Electric cables are carried under the floor of the bridge in concrete covered conduits hung from special steel stringers, which are supported upon the cross floor beams. The cement covering was crowned between the stringers to shed rain water and was reinforced with wire mesh. Duct manholes were built at the east shore pier and at the west river pier, fire-proofed on the interior.

At the east end the conduits are a continuation of the conduits built into the south wall of the Subway. They are carried under the outside tracks until they reach a junction chamber at the end of the main bridge span. At this point they cross to the inner tracks, under which they are carried at the level of the outside tracks.

The quantities of the principal items of construction on the work are as follows:

Excavation	3,209 cubic yards
Concrete	3,292 cubic yards
Stone masonry	2,001 cubic yards
Bolts and rods in caissons	65,540 pounds
Lumber in caissons	353,000 feet board measure
Temporary piles	145 piles
Lumber in temporary platforms	49,556 feet board measure
Structural steel in superstructure	1,383 tons

Work on the foundations of the Elevated Railway on West Market Street was begun on October 17, 1904.

The foundations are built of concrete, in the proportion of 100 pounds of cement, 3 cubic feet of fine gravel or coarse sand, and 6 parts of crushed stone. The standard piers, where good sand or gravel bottom was found, are truncated pyramids, 5 feet high, 4 feet by 4 feet at the top and 7 feet by 7 feet at the bottom, resting on a square base 8 feet by 8 feet in size and 1 foot 6 inches thick. Four anchor bolts $1\frac{3}{8}$ inches in diameter were built in each pier by which to secure the feet of the columns supporting the overhead structure. These bolts were inserted into 3 inch sheet steel tubes to facilitate final adjustment after the piers were built.

Over most of the line the soil under the footings consists of good sand or gravel with considerable inferior material where Market Street had been filled above the level of the original roadbed. In the latter case foundations comprise reinforced concrete plates upon which the pyramidal piers rest, the load per square foot on the soil being reduced to from 1 to $1\frac{1}{2}$ tons, and in exceptional cases, to less than 1 ton. Many of the piers on the western part of the line are founded on bed rock, which is relatively near the surface, the rock being excavated to a depth of 6 feet 6 inches as provision for the removal of the adjoining rock in the placing of sewers or other future underground structures.

Many pipes and sewers were encountered in the work, water and gas mains being carried through the concrete piers in sleeves to provide free space above and below the pipes to avoid breakage if settlement took place.

Between Thirty-third and Thirty-sixth Streets the foundations on the north side enclose and form a part of a sewer 4 feet 6 inches in diameter. In the latter case the brick sewer was cut out and replaced by concrete, so that the sewer forms a part of the pier.

Where Thirtieth Street passes under Market Street, the latter being supported upon a plate girder bridge, the foundations are built below the bed of Thirtieth Street, the Elevated Railway columns extending up through cast iron curbs in the deck of the bridge, so that no part of the column is in contact with the bridge. The construction of the foundations at Thirtieth Street required the underpinning of the old piers at the curb line of Thirtieth Street, which supports the bridge overhead, as the Elevated Railway foundations were close to the old piers and extended considerably below them.

The work comprises 785 foundations, including those for the stations, extending from the west end of the Schuylkill River Bridge to the end of the elevated structure near the Millbourne Mills.

The Elevated Railway comprises a two-track viaduct, on the centre line of Market Street; connected with the west end of the Schuylkill River Bridge by reverse curves on a radius of 420 feet, with transition ends. It extends in a straight line to a point west of Sixty-third Street.

The superstructure of the Elevated Railway differs from the elevated railways in other American cities, in the solid floor provided to prevent dripping into the street, and in the precautions taken to reduce the noise as much as possible. The steel floor is covered with concrete, on which is laid the rock ballast; cross ties are embedded in the ballast, supporting the running rails in the usual way with tie construction. The reduction of noise is quite satisfactory.

The first columns and girders of the superstructure were erected at Forty-fifth Street on August 22, 1905.

The structure is 19,377 feet long, comprising 18,697 feet of solid floor construction with cross ties and ballast, and 680 feet of open floor construction with cross ties laid upon deck girders. The main longitudinal girders are of lattice construction throughout except for 322 feet of plate girders on the reverse curve west of the Schuylkill River Bridge. There are eight passenger stations, located at the following streets, Thirty-second, Thirty-sixth, Fortieth, Forty-sixth, Fifty-second, Sixtieth, and Sixty-third. The length of spans is generally about 50 feet, with special lengths at the cross streets. The longest span is

W. H. SHELMERDINE
Director Philadelphia Rapid Transit Company

110 feet, at the crossing of the tracks of the Philadelphia and West Chester Traction Company on the West Chester Pike, opposite the Millbourne Mills.

The solid floor construction consists of riveted cross girders spaced 10 to 11 feet apart on the longitudinal lattice girders. On the upper flanges of the cross girders is supported a trough consisting of longitudinal "Z" bars with flat plates on the tops of the "Z" bars, and on the bottoms, plates with a flat longitudinal downward dish. The dish on the plates is used to collect possible seepage through the concrete bed, and conduct it to holes specially punched, having drips on their lower edges, thus avoiding the destruction of the paint by alkaline water. The steel floor is covered with Portland cement concrete in the proportion of 100 pounds cement, 3 parts of graded fine gravel or coarse sand and 6 parts graded crushed stone ranging from one-quarter inch to three-quarters inch in size. Upon the top of the concrete a granolithic mixture was placed before the concrete had set.

The concrete was reinforced with $\tfrac{3}{8}$ inch square deformed bars to resist shrinkage and temperature cracks and prevent leakage. The steel floor was painted with alkali resisting paint, an additional coat being given to the part of the floor where the concrete was thinnest, along the line of the middle drainage gutter. The rods were placed transversely 1 foot apart and longitudinally 18 inches apart. The concrete, having the fine and coarse aggregates well graded in size, and being deposited as wet as the conditions would allow, forms with the granolithic coating on top, and the steel reinforcement, a satisfactory protection of the steel floor. The concrete mixture was made not too rich so as not to induce shrinkage cracks.

To prevent slipping of the ballast on grades, checks or projections 1 inch high above the concrete, were built with granolithic surface, these checks being 6 inches wide and 12 inches long, spaced 1 foot 6 inches centre to centre. Two rows of the checks were placed in the bed under each track.

Drainage is provided by sloping the deck on 3 per cent. transverse grade downward toward a middle gutter. Longitudinal dams with scuppers form the gutter and retain the ballast in the bed of each track. The gutter has the same grade as the structure except where the latter is less than 1 per cent., no gutter grade having a grade of less than 1 per cent. The water is discharged at each column bent, and is conducted to collector boxes at the tops of the south columns, whence it passes to the street level by 3 inch cast iron soil pipes with a cast iron spout immediately above the fenders. At the stations all rain water from the roof and shelters and also from the roadway is conducted to the city sewers, underground longitudinal collector drains being placed where necessary.

The station platforms are 350 feet long, 250 feet being built to the permanent width of 10 feet 4 inches, and 50 feet at each end being made temporarily 4 feet wide without overhead shelter. The designs provide for shelters and platforms of the full width for the entire length of 350 feet. The shelters are supported by frames consisting of two light structural posts, the line of posts nearest the track being 4 feet 3 inches back from the edge of the platform and the posts furthest from the tracks being located in the lines of the railings. The posts are 20 feet apart centre to centre longitudinally, making very little obstruction to the platform. The standard station building is 57 feet 1 inch long and 17 feet 3 inches wide, comprising a waiting room at either end 19 feet by 9 feet in interior size, between which is the entrance lobby containing a ticket booth on each side of the entrance.

In each waiting room a toilet room has been provided with tiled floors and tiled wainscoting, and the best modern sanitary plumbing. The waiting rooms and ticket booths are heated by electric heaters.

The exterior of the buildings is covered with copper, and all roofs received felt, pitch and slag covering, except the steep shelters over the stairways, where the roofs are of tin.

The elevation of the station platforms above the sidewalk averages about 30 feet. Four stairways, at each of the four street corners, give access to the stations. The stairways leading from the street are 5 feet 8 inches wide, certain stairways in special situations being wider. All stairways are sub-divided by landings, the maximum number of risers in a flight being fourteen and the landings being usually 5 feet long. One foot-bridge has been built under the structure at each station, so that passengers may reach either the east or the west bound platforms without crossing on the street surface.

Open hearth steel of about 60,000 pounds ultimate strength was used for the entire structure, and all field riveting was done by pneumatic hammers. The material was painted one coat at the shop and two coats after erection. Expansion joints are placed in the structure about 200 feet apart, including usually 4 spans.

The main structure was erected with two travelers and two crews, one working from the western end, near Sixty-third Street toward Forty-fifth Street, and the other carrying on the work from Forty-fifth Street to join the Schuylkill River Bridge. Travelers moving forward on runways on the steel deck were used, having two steel booms 65 feet long. The framing to which the booms were connected consisted of two vertical posts with X-bracing between them, each vertical post supported by a stiff back leg attached to the framing of the traveling platform. Erection was finally completed on July 14, 1906, with the joining of the east and west sections at Forty-fifth Street.

The first train to run from the Sixty-ninth Street Terminal over the Elevated Railway and the Schuylkill River Bridge to the Fifteenth Street Subway station made the trip on Sunday morning, January 13, 1907.

The railway was opened to public travel on the morning of Monday, March 17, 1907, with trains of two cars operating on five minute headway between Sixty-ninth Street and

HENRY PHIPPS
Director Philadelphia Rapid Transit Company

Rotary Converters, Sansom Street Substation
Generators, Thirty-fourth and Market Streets

Exterior of Delaware Avenue Power Plant
Interior of Delaware Avenue Power Plant

Fifteenth Street, not stopping at the uncompleted stations at Thirty-sixth, Forty-sixth, and Sixty-third Streets.

The quantities of the principal items of construction are as follows:

Excavation	31,000	cubic yards
Concrete in foundations	10,377	cubic yards
Concrete in deck	10,000	cubic yards
Reinforcing rods in concrete deck	141	tons
Structural steel and iron work:		
Main superstructure, steel 23,048.6 tons		
Pipe railing fence (32,800 lineal feet) 210.4 tons		
Drainage appurtenances 64.6 tons		
Foundation grillages and bolts 183.7 tons		
Duct bridge over Thirtieth Street. 6.0 tons		
	23,507.3	tons

The tracks of the East Market Street Subway, after turning northward on the curve near the intersection of Market and Front Streets, emerge through two portals and ascend on an incline of 5 per cent., to meet the Delaware Avenue Elevated Railway. This begins at the intersection of Arch and Water Streets and extends eastward to Delaware Avenue, and thence southward along Delaware Avenue to the South Street terminus. The incline is built on property purchased by the Company, occupying a narrow tract 637 feet 9 inches long between Front and Water Streets from the south building line of Arch Street to the north line of the second property from Market Street. All the buildings on this tract, many of them old warehouses identified with the early commercial history of the city, were razed.

The Millard Construction Company began work June 20, 1907. The work includes retaining walls and a reinforced concrete viaduct about 290 feet long, having a concrete abutment at the northern end to receive the girders of the Elevated Railway, and one at its southern end. From the southern abutment a cut and fill extends between concrete retaining walls, since the grade of the roadbed intersects and descends below the grade of Water Street on the east (from 18 to 20 feet below Front Street) to meet the grade of the Subway tracks at the portals. The construction work also included tearing down part of the old buildings, the building of foundations for a future building over the incline, drains and connections to the sewers, and a reinforced concrete sidewalk on Front Street over old vaults which occupied a large proportion of the space under the easterly sidewalk of Front Street.

Filbert Street, an 8 foot passageway for pedestrians, was closed by authority of Councils and made the site of the abutment at the south end of the concrete viaduct.

Front Street is so much higher than Water Street that the second stories of the properties facing on Water Street formed the cellars on the Front Street side. Foundations for the new concrete walk on Front Street were made as follows: Between Arch Street and the abutment on the site of Filbert Street, the old cellar walls along the east building line of Front Street were braced against the cross walls of the viaduct. South of this point a retaining wall 83 feet 6 inches long was built; and thence south to the portals the old masonry was stripped of the upper instable portion and was rebuilt and masked by a new brick wall.

The viaduct is arranged to utilize the headroom beneath the railway for storage or other purposes, the cross walls and railway floor forming transverse chambers. The two southerly chambers contain one of the air compressor plants for the signal service.

The viaduct consists of a floor slab 12½ inches deep, supported upon cross walls 2 feet thick with openings in the walls 6 feet to 7 feet 9 inches wide between the chambers. The walls are spaced 15 feet 3 inches centre to centre. They are reinforced both vertically and horizontally to resist flexural stresses and to prevent shrinkage cracks.

The track on the viaduct is laid with cross ties and ballast; the track south of the viaduct is supported upon longitudinal concrete walls, one under each rail, the surface between and below the rails being covered with concrete, and the rails carried on channels, as in the Subway. The walls were built below the rails to avoid settlement, as the earth fill might otherwise have produced dangerous inequalities in the track at the juncture of the solid floor on the viaduct and the fill to the south.

A brick parapet wall 6 feet high has been built along the house lines of Arch, Front and Water Streets, to exclude trespassers. Gangways are provided on both sides of the viaduct on reinforced concrete cantilever construction, protected by pipe railings.

The alignment of the tracks, beginning at the portals of the Subway, comprises the north ends of the transition curves leading from the Subway, whence the track is on tangent for about 347 feet, after which the line passes to the right, the sharpest curves of the inside rails for the east bound and west bound tracks having respective radii of 129.32 and 143.32 feet, with transition ends. The superelevation of rail on the curves is 5 inches on both the east bound and west bound tracks.

The material in excavation was good sand and gravel, in agreement with the results of preliminary borings, and no unusual methods were required on the work.

The quantities of the principal items of construction are as follows:

Excavation	1,396 cubic yards
Concrete	3,303 cubic yards
Reinforcing rods for concrete	63 tons
Structural steel and iron	5 tons
Granolithic sidewalk	1,264 cubic yards
Earth fill	3,479 cubic yards

The Elevated Railway on Arch Street and Delaware Avenue leads from the incline between Market and Arch Streets to the eastern terminus of the Market Street system,

JEROME H. LOUCHHEIM
President Millard Construction Company

Rail Bond to Channel Plate Single Span Roof, East Market Street Subway
Shoring up Buildings, Constructing East Market Street Subway Automatic Coupling of Cars

Delaware Avenue Elevated Railway
Subway Portal, Front and Market Streets

West Market Street Elevated Railway
Incline on Front Street, from the Portal to Arch Street

at South Street, with a total length of 4,161 feet. The structure begins at a concrete abutment at the northern end of the reinforced concrete viaduct, and extends thence by curve of 138.41 feet radius on the centre line for a distance of 403 feet along Arch Street to a point on Delaware Avenue about 144 feet south of the south house line of Arch Street. After rounding the curve into Delaware Avenue, the tracks diverge to 40 feet 9 inches centre to centre to embrace the island platform for the passenger station which extends from Market to Chestnut Streets. From Chestnut Street southward the structure is 40 feet 9 inches wide, a third track having been built in the centre to the South Street Terminal, which also has an island platform. The length of the third track is 1,795 feet, exclusive of the cross-overs. This portion of the line was opened to traffic as far as Market and Chestnut Streets on September 7, 1908.

On the curve, 403 feet from Water and Arch Streets to Delaware Avenue, the structure has a solid floor like the West Market Street Elevated. Along Delaware Avenue the floor is open, with cross ties laid on the top flanges of the girders.

The foundations for the columns are all of concrete, and are supported on piles, since the entire bed of Delaware Avenue is made ground. The row of columns nearest the Delaware River is built on the portion of Delaware Avenue as widened in 1900. The surface of the street is supported on pile and timber platform decking. The expensive nature of the foundations led to the adoption of spans averaging 75 feet in length, the longest being 85 feet. The number of piles in the foundations varies from twelve to thirty-six. Upon the tops of the pile foundations reinforced concrete piers were founded, reinforcement in the concrete platforms providing for equal distribution of the load over the piles in each foundation.

To prevent distortion of the columns, due to lateral movement of the pile foundations owing to possible gradual settlement of the artificial bed of the street, steel tie rods were placed transversely between each pair of columns.

The curved structure at Arch Street comprises three lines of longitudinal lattice girders supported on transverse plate girders which rest on columns in the sidewalk near the curb lines. This portion of the structure is irregular, owing to the curvature and grades. The cross girders are 6 feet $8\frac{1}{2}$ inches deep over chord angles; the longest girder, extending over Arch Street on the east line of Water Street, is 69 feet long and weighs 50,000 pounds.

The open deck structure has a pair of lattice girders under each track. These girders are 6 feet $11\frac{1}{4}$ inches in depth, the longest deck girder being 85 feet long and weighing 25,900 pounds. Some other longitudinal girders exceed this in weight, the heaviest being 43,500 pounds. The section of the top chords of the longitudinal girders was so composed as to avoid cover plates, rivet heads and other interference with the placing of cross ties.

Two stations have been built, one reaching from Market to Chestnut Street, and the other at South Street.

The station between Market and Chestnut Streets has a passenger platform 352 feet 3 inches long, exclusive of the space occupied by the waiting rooms, and 31 feet 4 inches wide. As a part of the work of building this station, the 150 foot span extending across Delaware Avenue from stairways at the foot of Chestnut Street and leading to the Recreation Pier, was removed and replaced by a new bridge 10 feet and 21 feet wide west and east of the Elevated Railway structure, respectively. The new bridge serves as a passenger entrance to the Chestnut Street end of the station, the stairways at the foot of Chestnut Street remaining as originally built. The bridge also furnishes connection to the ferry at the foot of Chestnut Street. From the bridge a main stairway 22 feet 10 inches wide, divided into three passageways by intermediate handrails, leads to the level of a lobby or underpassage, the middle passage leading to the ticket office and waiting room on the level of the train platform. The two outer passages on the main stairway form the exits from the underpassage, which is reached by two stairways from the train platform north of the waiting room.

At the Market Street end of the station two stairways have been built, each 5 feet $1\frac{1}{2}$ inches wide, on the north and south sidewalks respectively of Market Street. Each stairway is connected by a foot bridge to a lobby below the train platform, whence a main entrance stairway 22 feet wide leads to the ticket office and waiting room, which are on the level of the train platform. South of and under the main entrance stairway, an exit stairway has been built 21 feet 3 inches wide, leading from a passageway under the train platform, passengers descending from the train platform by two stairways, each 4 feet 9 inches wide.

From the easterly side of the lobby a passageway 21 feet 5 inches in width extends to the ferry at the foot of Market Street, descent to the street level at the ferry house being made by two 8 foot stairways at right angles to the passageway.

Owing to a requirement of the franchise ordinance the clear height of the elevated structure over the steam railroad tracks is 20 feet. As the tracks are placed on the top flanges of the longitudinal girders, the space beneath the train platform and the track girders has been utilized for the lobbies at the extremities of the station, and the designs provide for the future connection of the lobbies by underpassages extending from Market Street to Chestnut Street, with additional exit stairways from the train platform to provide for the rapid discharge of crowds when traffic is heavy.

All of the platforms and stairways on both stations are built of Ferro-Inclave construction, having a total thickness of $2\frac{3}{8}$ inches, the top consisting of concrete made with Portland cement, sand, and trap rock grit. The bottom is plastered with mortar, by which means all parts of the sheet steel composing the Ferro-Inclave base are protected from rust.

On all steps and at the edges of the train platform, carborundum safety treads have been placed to prevent slipping. Along the edges of all train platforms, owing to the exposed situation of the platforms, sections of pipe railing have been placed, arranged with openings to permit free access of passengers to the end and middle doors of the cars.

The station buildings have steel framework, the exterior of the sides being covered with copper, including cornices and mouldings. The interior finish and furnishings of the stations is of red oak with natural finish. All roofing, except on the steep pitch of the shelters over the stairways, is of granulated slag on felt sheathing. The roofs over the stairways are covered with tin.

The station at the terminus at South Street has an island platform 31 feet 4 inches wide, and 330 feet long, to which access is furnished by a foot-bridge from the westerly sidewalk of Delaware Avenue near South Street, which is served by two stairways each 5 feet 6 inches in width, and parallel to Delaware Avenue. Provision has been made in the design for a connection to the ferries at the foot of South Street.

The style of details is similar to that of the station between Chestnut and Market Streets, the tracks being laid upon the top flanges of the girders and the space below the train platform being utilized for a lobby and underpassage. Passengers enter the station by the foot bridge and stairway on the west sidewalk of Delaware Avenue and pass thence to a lobby beneath the train platform, to which access from the ferries will also be made in the future. Two exit stairways have been built, one leading from the train platform north of the waiting room to the underpassage to the lobby, and one leading from the train platform south of the waiting room direct to the floor of the lobby.

Owing to interference with an old ferry house, which protrudes within the proposed widened line of Delaware Avenue, the end span of the main structure has been omitted, over which the station structure is intended to ultimately extend. A temporary frame building has been erected at the southerly end of the station for temporary toilet conveniences. The shelter of the passenger platform has been erected over three of the spans included within the station and will be extended in the future to cover the remaining two spans at the north end. A signal tower has been built at the north end of the platform to control switches and the movement of trains.

The construction of the waiting room, which includes the ticket offices, is similar to that for the station between Market and Chestnut Streets.

Work was started on the foundations at South Street on July 31, 1906, and completed in June, 1907. The work of setting the column bases, concreting about the feet of the columns, building the steps at the feet of the stairways on the sidewalk, and other miscellaneous work, began on September 23, 1907, and was completed in June, 1908.

Erection of the main structure began on September 8, 1907, with the erection of the columns on the east side of Water Street to support the girder spanning Arch Street at this point. Erection proceeded until November 5, 1907, and was resumed on January 10, 1908, then continuing without interruption until May 28, 1908, when the last girder was raised. Riveting was completed on June 9, 1908. The erection of the main structure was done with a traveler having two booms 90 feet long stayed to vertical steel posts with stiff timber back legs, and mounted on a timber platform, the traveler being widened as erection proceeded from Arch Street south to include the widened structure, where the tracks spread around the island platforms.

The erection of the structural steel for the stations and stairways began with the canopy at Market Street, on March 30, 1908, and the superstructure of the stations on the structural frame work began at Market Street July 13, 1908.

The principal items of construction are as follows:

Excavation	10,000 cubic yards
Concrete	4,560 cubic yards
Piles in foundations	2,864 piles
Reinforcing rods for concrete	100 tons
Anchor bolts	11 tons
Structural steel work:	
Main structure .... 5,912 tons	
Station steel .... 199 tons	
	6,111 tons
Pipe rail fence	9,162 lineal feet

Train Yards, Sixty-ninth Street Terminal
Repair Shops, Sixty-ninth Street Terminal

Department Store Window, East Market Street Subway

ARTHUR LOEB
Vice-President Millard Construction Company

TRACK CONSTRUCTION: THIRD RAIL: SIGNAL AND TELEPHONE SYSTEMS

THE Elevated structure between Twenty-ninth Street and Sixty-third Street is provided with a solid steel trough floor, upon which is placed a reinforced concrete deck or covering with a rough granolithic finish. The top surface of the concrete is formed on a 3 per cent. grade sloping from the sides toward the centre, along which line is a drainage gutter with outlet pipes at each cross girder. The sides of this gutter are formed of concrete with "weep" holes at frequent intervals. The gutter is covered with reinforced concrete slabs built in sections 12 inches long so that they may be readily removed for the purpose of cleaning out the gutter. The top of the concrete is at such a height that it will allow a minimum depth of $5\frac{5}{8}$ inches of ballast under the outer edge of the ties; this increasing to about $8\frac{1}{4}$ inches at the inner edge. The ballast is composed of first-class trap rock uniformly 1 inch size. It is carried to the tops of the ties throughout, covering completely the central drain.

The ties are 6 inches by 8 inches by 8 feet, sawed chestnut and oak, and spaced $22\frac{1}{2}$ inches centre to centre, giving sixteen ties for each 30 foot rail. The rails are in 30 foot lengths and of Bessemer steel, the A. S. C. E. 90 pound section. They are secured to the ties by means of clips and screw spikes. In order to facilitate the work of placing, the ties were all drilled to templet for the screw spikes before being placed on the structure. All that was necessary to secure the track in position was to place the clips and screw down the spikes. These spikes were of special design, $5\frac{1}{2}$ inches long under the head, $\frac{3}{4}$ inch in diameter at the root of the threads and 1 inch in diameter where the spike passes through the clip. Weber joint plates are used to connect the rails; they are six-hole plates 32 inches in length.

As an element of safety an inside guard rail is placed along each rail for the entire length of the structure, forming a throat of 4 inches between guard and running rails. It is connected to the running rail by bolts and adjustable chocks at intervals of about six feet. This rail also is secured to the ties by screw spikes and the joints in the guard rail are laid to break joints with the running rail. In establishing the width of throat at 4 inches, it was thought advisable so to place the guard rail that, if possible, the wheels of the truck should not be allowed to leave the rails entirely from any tendency to derailment. That is, for instance, should a broken flange, or other cause, tend to throw the wheels to the right, the back of the flanges on the left hand wheel would engage the guard rail before the tread of the left hand wheel had completely left the running rail, and before the flange of the right hand wheel had cleared the running rail on that side, thereby keeping trucks in reasonable alignment until the train could be brought to a standstill. It might be added that the top of the separating chocks is of sufficient depth below head of rail to provide clearance for worn wheels with deep flanges.

The third rail is carried by wooden arms extending under the sidewalk and is entirely free from the track structure. Part of the track has been in operation for upwards of eighteen months and no difficulty has been experienced in maintaining the proper relation between running rail and third rail.

Between Sixty-third Street and private right-of-way west of Millbourne Mills, the ties are laid directly on the chord members of the trusses, there being no solid floor in this short section. The ties are securely anchored to the steel work by means of hook bolts passing through the ties and the running rail, and the guard rails are secured to these ties in the same manner as on the ballasted section. From Millbourne Mills to the Terminal at Sixty-ninth Street, track is on private right-of-way. The subgrade was graded to give a depth of 8 inches for ballast under the ties. The same kind of ties and the same construction is used on this part of the track as on the ballasted portion of the Elevated, excepting that the safety guard is omitted, and the third rail is carried on long ties.

The switches and frogs of special work are made of manganese steel; switches being of the split switch type but of a special design with the points of solid manganese. The economy in this type of switch has been fully demonstrated during the past eighteen months of service.

On plain curves, with a radius of between 500 and 600 feet, the inside rail is provided with a manganese steel working guard of a section similar to the safety guard used on the straight track, but heavier. This guard is set so as to give a throat of $1\frac{3}{4}$ inches, thereby engaging the back flange of the inside wheels against this guard rail, and reducing the wear on the outside running rail. On curves under 500 feet in radius, both inside and outside rails are provided with a working guard of this type; the outside rail, however, being of the rolled guard section while the inner guard rail is of manganese steel. On the reverse curves at Twenty-ninth and Market Streets there has been placed an additional tee rail guard inside of the working guard, as an additional precaution against possible accident from derailment.

The track work on the third rail portion of the Delaware Avenue Elevated, which extends from Chestnut to South Streets, is somewhat different. The structure in this section has an open floor, with the ties laid directly on the top chords of the trusses. As these trusses are spaced 8 feet from centre to centre, it was necessary to use a somewhat deeper tie in order to give the desired strength. The ties in this section are made of 8 inch by 10 inch by 10 feet

Sixty-ninth Street Terminal. Train Shed Above; Waiting Room Below

Views in and about the Sixty-ninth Street Terminal Yards

JAMES P. McNICHOL
Treasurer Millard Construction Company

first quality yellow pine and creosoted. Before delivery these ties were dressed to 9 inches in the middle of the tie and 10 inches at the ends. This extra depth at the end was provided in order to facilitate surfacing the ties to conform to the slight irregularities on the surface of the iron work. The ties are spaced the usual distance, that is, sixteen ties to a 30 foot rail, and each tie is secured to the chord by means of four $\frac{3}{4}$ inch hook bolts passing through the tie with their lower end shaped to conform to the under side of the bulb angles. Every fifth tie is made 10 feet 6 inches long, and on these ties is carried the third rail bracket. The rail is the same as used on the Elevated structure on West Market Street, and is secured to the ties in the same manner. Instead of using the "Z" bar section of safety guard, however, standard tee rail of the same section as the running rail has been used for this purpose, and in order to secure the proper space between the base of rails for the fastenings, it was necessary to increase the throat $\frac{3}{8}$ inch, making it $4\frac{3}{8}$ inches instead of 4 inches. This distance, however, is still small enough to prevent complete derailment of the wheels.

The special work in this section is practically the same as is used throughout the entire Elevated system. But it might be added, that all the special work is so designed that all switches are interchangeable; that is, any right hand switch of this design can be placed in any right hand location throughout the entire Subway and Elevated system (with the exception, of course, of the unbroken main-line emergency cross-overs), thus reducing the number of pieces that must be carried for emergency purposes.

With the exception of the Delaware Avenue Elevated and the short section of private right-of-way at the western end, no joints in the running rail are bonded for return circuit. In the Subway the anchoring channels are bonded and the centre of each rail connected to these channels. On the Elevated structure, the steel work of the structure itself is bonded, and the centre of the running rail bonded to the steel work. The rail of the running track, which is used for signaling purposes, is, however, connected with light bond wires for this purpose.

In the construction of the Subway roadbed, the use of concrete for the purpose may be said to have been established. There is not a yard of ballast from one end of the Subway to the other.

Concrete was first used tentatively for fifteen months on Subway tracks carrying single heavy eight wheel two truck cars on about a three minute headway. Following this the same construction was adopted on about 7,000 feet of track carrying trains of three or four steel-framed cars operating on a four minute headway. The complete success of this second trial, extending over a year and more of actual service, left no doubt as to its adaptability for the service. The principal point of difference between this construction and all others lies in the fact that the ties rest directly on the concrete and not on the channels which form the anchors. The cost of maintenance was practically nothing, beyond the wages of two track walkers, one night and one day, part of whose time was spent in sweeping up accumulations of dust, etc.

The structure for each track consists of four 12 inch 20½ pound channels, arranged in pairs, one pair under each rail. The channels are placed back to back in pairs, and are held 15 inches apart by separators, which consist of 4 inch sections of 15 inch channels, riveted at intervals to the webs of the 12 inch channels. Concrete is then placed inside each pair and leveled up ⅛ inch above the upper surface of the channels, to form a concrete bearing surface for the ties; and the spaces between the rails and outside them is also filled up with concrete.

Laying the tracks proceeded as follows: The 12 inch channels were provided in 30 foot lengths, the webs drilled with the necessary holes for the rivets of the separater channels; and the upper flanges drilled with holes for the tie bolts, two holes for each tie, so spaced as to bolt each tie by diagonally opposite corners. Having been assembled in pairs, the channels were deposited in the Subway, put into approximate place and coupled up.

Rail in 60-foot lengths had already been distributed. The rail is 90-pound, A. S. C. E. type. Manganese steel is used on curves.

The channels were then assembled by temporary ties, which were long enough to hold both pairs of channels, and had been previously drilled to templet with holes for the bolts to the channels and for the screw spikes to the rails. This ensures the proper relation between the channel, the tie, and the rail.

These temporary ties were spaced 7½ feet apart and were bolted to the channels. The rails are then placed and spiked to the ties, and the assembled group of channels, ties, and rails is wedged into true line and surface.

A 1:3:6 concrete was then filled into the 15 inch space between each pair of channels, and brought up to within 3 inches of the finished top surface. This was allowed to set long enough to hold the channels securely against possible movement, when the rails and temporary ties were removed. The rails were laid aside until wanted for permanent placement, while the ties were moved ahead to another section.

The top concrete surface is a 1:2:4 mixture of cement, sand, and trap rock grit, placed before the first layer has entirely set. It is brought to a level ⅛ inch above the top surface of the channels, the wooden surfacing tools being guided by ⅛ inch metal strips clamped to the top of the channels.

The space between and outside the tracks was concreted. The surface slopes slightly away from the tracks in each direction, being 2½ inches below the bottom of the ties at the channels.

Permanent ties were bolted into position after the concrete was thoroughly hardened. The ties are 6 inches by 10 inches by 2 feet, surfaced to 5⅞ inches exactly. They were spaced

2 feet centre to centre, and were laid directly on the concrete. Two bolt holes were drilled in each tie with gang drills, in diagonally opposite corners. Bolts are ¾ inch diameter, passing through the ties and the upper flanges of the channels. They are inserted head up and are fastened by a cast iron nut that conforms to the under surface of the flange.

The space about the upper flanges of the channels and the cast iron nuts was then filled up with cement mortar. In the finished roadbed only the upper surface of the channels shows.

Holes for the rail spikes were drilled in the ties by pneumatic drills driven by portable compressors, or by air from the signal system, which had already been placed. The spike does not bear directly on the rail base, but on a cast iron clip, which gives a better bearing and prevents the base of the rail from cutting the spike.

The construction on the curves is similar, except that the channels are bent to the proper radii, and the holes are drilled so as to put the ties in a radial position. Needed super-elevation is taken care of in placing the channels, obviating the necessity for wedge-shaped ties.

The trials made of this construction indicated, as shown above, that absolute permanence had been secured. The rails and ties, on which all the wear comes, are readily replaced, without interfering with traffic. But the very indestructibility of the foundation reduces wear, and makes negligible the maintenance expense due to faults of lining and surfacing. The rails are so securely anchored to their foundations that creeping and vibration are lessened, joints keep in better condition, and rail corrugations are minimized. The foundation being homogeneous, each tie takes its full share of the load, which is much more evenly distributed than with any other construction. Perfect cleanliness is easily maintained, as the whole Subway can be flushed out if necessary, water draining off rapidly.

Electrically, also, the Subway-Elevated tracks are unique. Early in the construction of the road it was decided to avoid, if possible, the bonding of rail joints, on account of the difficulty in maintaining such bonding. By utilizing the channels under the Subway track and the metal of the Elevated structure this was easily accomplished.

In the Subway the channels were bonded with soldered bonds, having a total cross-section of 4,000,000 circ. mils. These channels gave a total cross-section $2\frac{1}{2}$ times that of the 90 pound rail. Each rail length was bonded to this supplemental return with a 300,000 circ. mil cable bond compressed into the base of the rail by means of a hydraulic tool, the hole being punched by the same means. Four 2,250,000 circ. mil cables were extended from the Sansom Street Substation to the Subway and tapped into the channel system at Seventh and Market Streets.

On the Elevated structure the longitudinal girders were bonded with compressed terminal bonds, having a total cross-section of 4,000,000 circ. mils. Each rail length on the return rail was connected to the structure by a 300,000 circ. mil cable bond, compressed into the base of the rail as in the Subway. Connections were made to the Elevated structure at the Thirty-third and Market Streets Power House and at the Allison and Market Streets Substation.

A bull-head rail is used, hung on porcelain insulators and giving contact to the shoe from the under surface.

The third rail is hung entirely independent of the track structure by either of two methods, cutting down vibration to a minimum and preventing the breaking of porcelain insulators. In the East Section of the Subway the insulators are hung from a cast iron bracket bolted to a support tie and resting on the same concrete bed as the track tie. But the support tie is surfaced off a trifle thinner than the track tie so that it does not touch the running rail. On the Elevated and the West Section of the Subway the insulators are hung from malleable iron castings carried on wooden cross-arms which are bolted to the Elevated structure or to the columns in the Subway.

Protective coverings of vulcanized fiber are used in the East Section. In the West Section and the Elevated a three-piece wooden covering is used.

The under surface of the third rail is 6 inches above the head of the running rail, and its centre line is 27 inches outside the gauge line of the track.

The third rail is bonded at each joint with two 500,000 circ. mil compressed terminal bonds, a hydraulic tool being used to upset the terminals. The third rail feeders are of 2,000,000 circ. mil cross-section. These feeders are brought from the substation to a cast iron switch box, near the point where they are to tap into the rail. A 1,500,000 circ. mil cable is used from the switch box to the rail itself. All of these boxes are placed in a convenient place, so that a cable can be cut out with the least possible delay if necessary. The sectional breaks are jumped by means of 1,500,000 circ. mil cables through one of these switch boxes.

On the East Section and the City Hall loop a three-quarter minute headway can be maintained. The signal system on the Market Street Elevated and Subway is of the electro-pneumatic type. On the section west of the City Hall the signals are arranged for minimum headway of one and one-half minutes.

There is no overlap on the East Section, although similar results are accomplished by placing the setting point of each signal beyond the signal itself by a distance equal to the braking distance of a train with an emergency application of the brakes. On the Western Section a one block overlap is used, except at the approaches to the stations, where the overlap is removed by means of a cut section. This allows a train to follow within one block of a station while the preceding train is standing in the station. As there are no express trains the distant blade is omitted on the signal approaching each station.

On the Elevated an iron pole semaphore signal is used, the bottom blade being 15 feet above the base. In the Subway an electric light signal is used, having no moving parts, the lamps being lit and turned out by means of a direct current relay. Electro-pneumatic train stops are used throughout the entire line. While the signals are normal clear the stops are normal danger.

The signals are operated primarily from a closed track circuit, which is energized by alternating current furnished from transformers along the line. These transformers have a primary winding for 1,100 volts, and two secondary windings, one to supply the track circuit at 10 volts and another to supply the current for lighting the signals at 55 volts. The return circuit is through one of the running rails, which is divided into blocks for the signal system. The 10 volt alternating current is fed into one end of the block through a cast iron grid resistance, which can be adjusted to suit the local conditions of the block it is to feed. An alternating current relay is bridged across the two rails of the track at the opposite end of the block from the track feed. This relay will respond only to alternating current. Its windings, however, would be subject to the heating effects of return direct current were it not for a low resistance impedance coil which is bridged across the terminals of the alternating current relay and shunts out the direct current from the relay, at the same time offering enough impedance to prevent any appreciable shunting of the alternating current.

A pair of battery mains at 14 volts is extended the entire length of the line. It is fed by six sets of storage cells which are kept charged from the third rail. This battery current is used in actuating all magnetic valves on the pneumatic movements and also for actuating the direct current relays to light the Subway signals.

The operation of the block system may be briefly described as follows: Alternating current is fed into the leaving end of a block and is taken from the entering end of the block to an alternating current relay. When a train enters the block the presence of an axle between the rails of the track shunts the alternating current relay, de-energizing it and breaking its secondary contact.

The secondary contact circuit is from the 14 volt battery mains through the magnetic valves on the cylinders of the signal mechanism. The breaking of this contact de-energizes the magnet valve, allowing the air pressure in the cylinder to exhaust. A counterweight on the signal blade then draws the blade to the danger position by the action of gravity. The movement of this blade is repeated to the distant blade through a wire extending back one block.

As a train leaves the block the shunting action of the axle is removed. The alternating current relay is again picked up, closing its secondary circuit; this in turn energizes the magnet valve, applying air to the cylinder, which draws the blade to the clear position against the action of the counterweight. It is apparent that the breaking of any wire or the failure of air pressure will cause the signal to fall to the danger position. The only possible causes for a clear failure are a defective alternating current relay, or foreign current applied directly to the magnet valve circuit.

Air pressure is supplied at 90 pounds to the square inch, through a 2 inch galvanized iron pipe which extends the entire length of the line. This pipe is supplied from three sources. At the Terminal there are two steam driven air compressors; at Thirty-third and Market Streets there are two steam driven compressors, and at Front and Arch Streets there are two compressors driven by 600 volt direct current electric motors. Each of these compressors has a capacity of 250 cubic feet of free air per minute. It will be noted that each compressor station is provided with duplicate sets, in order to provide against failure of any one machine. Under normal working conditions one of these compressors will supply enough air for all signals, train stops, and switches, the excess capacity being provided to take care of any drain on the line which might be caused by leaks or by the use of pneumatic tools in track construction or structural steel work. It might be added that the use of this compressed air has been found a great convenience as well as a saving of time and money in the operation of these pneumatic tools.

All switches on this road are operated from electro-pneumatic interlocking plants. These are located at the terminals, also at the cross-overs at Fifty-second, Twenty-ninth, Fifteenth, Eighth and Second Streets. There are also two interlocking plants at the City Hall to control the switches at that point. Alternating current bar track circuits are used at all switches, no mechanical detector bars being used.

The Philadelphia Rapid Transit Company operates a telephone system which centralizes at its office building at Eighth and Dauphin Streets. All the properties of the Company are connected by this exchange by its own underground telephone wires. In view of the individual character of the Subway and Elevated system it was decided to place a branch exchange at the Sixty-ninth Street Terminal, connecting it to Eighth and Dauphin Streets by trunks, and having all the telephones connected with the Elevated and Subway system operate from the branch exchange at the Terminal. A 110 pair lead covered and paper insulated cable was installed from the Sixty-ninth Street Terminal to Delaware Avenue. Another 110 pair cable was installed from Twelfth and Market Streets to Thirteenth and Mount Vernon Streets, where connection is made with other cables leading to the Eighth and Dauphin Streets exchange. At Twelfth and Market Streets a large junction box is installed where cross connections can be made between any pairs in these cables, leading north, east, and west. Each station along the line is provided with a telephone in each ticket booth. There are also a number of telephones distributed along the line in cast iron boxes for the use of track walkers, signal men and inspectors.

CHARLES Q. MacDONOUGH
Secretary Millard Construction Company

Department Store Windows, East Market Street Subway

Department Store Entrance, East Market Street Subway
Cross-over to Sub-level Station, Thirteenth Street

ROLLING STOCK AND EQUIPMENT

THE Elevated-Subway service requires from eighty to one hundred cars. At the slack hours fourteen trains of two cars each are in use; and at the rush hours fourteen trains of five cars each. The number of trains per hour and of cars per train are to be increased as traffic warrants it.

Before deciding upon the type of cars a thorough investigation was made of the different designs in use on other rapid transit systems, both in this country and abroad. A steel-framed car of the design developed and used by the Boston Elevated Railroad Company appeared the best to answer Philadelphia conditions, and with some slight modifications was adopted.

These cars are of substantially all steel construction,—woodwork being used only for the interior finish, which is of mahogany. The entire underframe is of steel, and the floor is a monolithic composition laid on corrugated sheets. Seats are of cane. They run lengthwise the side of the car, from each corner toward the central door, which is left free for the exit of passengers. The seating capacity is forty-four.

In order to avoid accidents through carelessness in putting an arm or head out of the window, the windows are arranged to lower from the top only several inches, giving ample ventilation while guarding the lower part of the opening. There is also a row of ventilators along the clerestory on each side. Passengers enter through the end doors, and leave through the centre doors, all of which are operated by compressed air controlled by the trainmen from the ends of the car. Lighting is done by 16 candle-power lamps in the centre line of the ceiling and along the sides.

On account of the requirements of the ordinance, that stations shall average not more than one-half mile apart, it was not deemed feasible to attempt a greater schedule speed than fifteen to sixteen miles per hour, and even this assumption was based on station stops not exceeding twenty seconds each. Furthermore, heavy grades seemed to indicate that the best results would be obtained by making each car a motor car, and accordingly on one truck of each car are mounted two General Electric No. 66 motors, rated at 125 horse-power each. The armature of these motors carries a 17 tooth pinion. The axle gear has 61 teeth, $2\frac{1}{2}$ inch pitch. The frames of both the motor and trailer trucks are interchangeable, having a uniform wheel base of 6 feet 7 inches.

General Electric-Sprague multiple unit system of control is used on all the cars. The whole train is controlled by the motorman on the front platform of the head car. The controller is so arranged that it automatically returns to its dead point should he take his hand from the handle. No train cable is used on either power or lighting circuits. The gaps in the third rail are consequently short and are not bridged by the train.

The Westinghouse Traction air brakes are equipped with electric control and gradual release. The air pumps are motor operated and supply air for both the brakes and the operation of the doors.

Heavy pattern Van Dorn car couplings with Westinghouse automatic couplers for the air pipes are used.

The overall height of the car (top of rail to top of car roof) was originally designed to be 12 feet 5 inches, but modifications in the trucks have since increased this to 13 feet, giving approximately one foot clearance between the roof of the car and the roof of the Subway.

	Motor Trucks	Trailer Trucks
Gauge of track	5 feet 2¼ inches	5 feet 2¼ inches
Wheel base	6 feet 7 inches	6 feet 7 inches
Weight on centre plate with loaded car	20,000 pounds	20,000 pounds
Centre bearings	Symington ball	Symington ball
Side bearings	Symington ball	Symington ball
Wheels (solid rolled steel)	34 inches	34 inches
Axles—centre diameter	6 inches	6 inches
Axles—gear seat	6½ inches	—
Axles—wheel seat	6½ inches	6½ inches
Journals	5 inches by 9 inches	5 inches by 9 inches
Journal boxes	Symington	Symington
Weight of trucks	21,500 pounds (with motors)	12,750 pounds
Weight of car body complete	34,300 pounds	

LIGHTING OF THE SUBWAY-ELEVATED SYSTEM: DRAINAGE

THE daytime lighting of the Subway stations is much simplified by the extensive use of vault lights in the sidewalks. Heavy glass lights are used, 70,000 being used in the Eighth Street station alone.

The artificial lighting throughout the Subway-Elevated system is done by 16 candle-power incandescent lamps.

From the portal at the Delaware River to the east side of City Hall, the Subway tunnel has a light every 60 feet on each side, the lights on one side being placed midway between those on the other; this gives a light for every 30 lineal feet, or 780 square feet of horizontal surface per lamp. Around the City Hall loop the lights are only 20 feet apart, but the tunnel is wider, so that each light has to illuminate 808 square feet. West of the City Hall the tunnel is four tracks wide and the lights are placed 25 feet apart, making about 1,150 square feet per light.

The station platforms are supplied with light on the basis of 32 to 38 square feet per lamp.

There are two methods of lighting used—by direct current at 550 volts for emergency service, and 25 cycle alternating current for regular service. Taps are made from the alternating current lighting cable at each station to a transformer placed in the transformer room at the western end of the south platform. The secondary of this transformer is to furnish power at 550 volts, and to be provided with four intermediate taps, making five circuits of 110 volts each. These circuits are connected to the fuse panel at each transformer, and a six conductor cable runs from here to each of the panel boards.

The panel boards have at the middle of the top a 6-pole double throw switch, the normal position of which would be up, connecting the six lines of the alternating current circuit to the six bus bars of the panel board. The two lower clips of the 6-pole switch are connected to a direct current lighting cable and to the ground respectively. On either side of the 6-pole switch is a single pole double throw switch. As there are four panel boards in each station there would be eight of these switches, and they are used to supply current to the tunnel lights, ticket offices, heaters, emergency lights, store entrances, etc.

At the bottom of each panel board are two sets of five switches, connected to the six bus bars. Each of these switches controls a circuit of ten lights wired in multiple. When the power for the lights is being taken from the alternating current circuit, with the 6-pole switch up, any one of the ten small switches may be closed, the same as on any 110 volt service. When the alternating current cable is out of service, the 6-pole switch is thrown down and all the ten switches may be closed, lighting all the lights, or any five switches may be closed so long as no two are opposite. The lamps would then be connected in series multiple.

The major portion of the lights at the stations are in clusters of five, and wired in multiple, so that two clusters make the necessary ten lights for one alternating current circuit. Every fourth cluster is wired in series and connects to the 550 volt direct current cable, and forms part of the emergency lighting.

There are so many lights in the Subway, and they cover so great an area for 110 volt service, that this system was devised. It gives 110 volt service on a high tension alternating current supply, through a step-down transformer whose secondary is 550 volts with 110 volt taps; and operates under emergency conditions on a 550 volt direct current supply.

All the wires in the stations are installed in loricated conduit, which is laid in the cement work. The lighting wires through the tunnels are held on heavy porcelain insulators attached to maple cross-arms. The maple cross-arms are bolted into a cast iron block, which is fastened to the side wall of the tunnel by lag screws and lead plugs.

The wiring of all the Elevated stations is laid out on the same general plan. The lights on each platform are controlled from a panel board in the ticket booth. At the bottom of the panel board is a double throw switch, the hinge point of which connects to the distributing bus bar of the panel board. The clip points connect to the lighting cable and third rail respectively through a service box placed under the floor of the platform at the nearest expansion joint to the station. In case of trouble on the lighting cable, this switch can be thrown over and all the lights in the station supplied from the third rail.

All the lights are connected five in series on a 550 volt circuit, so that five lamps go out if one lamp in the circuit burns out. To prevent the stairs from being in darkness should a circuit of lights burn out, the lights down the stairways are all double circuited. The waiting rooms are lighted by three circuits of lights.

The platforms are 10 feet wide, with a row of lights front and back. The two rows are about 6 feet apart, with a lamp every 16 feet, which figures about one lamp for every 80 square feet of platform. In the waiting rooms there is one lamp for every 22 square feet of floor space, and the toilet rooms have about the same.

All the electric heaters in the Elevated stations are of 3 ampere capacity, connected two in series on 550 volts, mounted on a slate base and protected by a wrought iron guard. There is one unit installed in each toilet room and ticket booth, and three units in each waiting room. This has been found to give very satisfactory heating, and is about 7.3

S. M. SWAAB
Engineer in Charge of Construction, Millard Construction Company

watts per cubic foot for the ticket offices, 3.8 watts per cubic foot for the toilet rooms, and 2.7 watts per cubic foot for the waiting rooms.

Inasmuch as it was decided to put the switchboards in the ticket booths, leaving the control of the various circuits to the ticket seller, a special panel board was devised so as to reduce to a minimum the liability of danger in operating the switches.

The switches are mounted on a marble base 9 feet by 2 feet 6 inches, and are Perkins 500 volt indicating snap switches. The base is supported 2 inches in front of a $1\frac{1}{4}$ inch slate slab, on which are mounted the 600 volt National Standard Type "B" fuses. The hinge clip of the double throw switch, above referred to, connects to the main distributing bar through a 600 volt Type "E" fuse. All the switches are connected to the main bar, and from here they connect to the circuit fuses. The panel board door has an opening in the centre, so that when closed it covers all the fuses and live points of the circuits, leaving exposed the marble base with the switches mounted thereon. To control any circuit it is only necessary to turn the handle of the snap switch. There is no occasion for opening the panel board doors, except by an experienced wireman in case of trouble with the circuits.

The drainage water in the Subway is collected at four different points. From the west portal at the Schuylkill River the drainage is carried in two 12 inch terra cotta pipes to a sump well at Twenty-second Street, and from Sixteenth Street west to the same well through two 12 inch terra cotta pipes.

From Sixteenth Street eastward the drainage water is carried to a sump at Fifteenth Street, and from the south side of City Hall westward to the same sump.

The north side of City Hall drains eastward to a sump at Juniper Street; and from Thirteenth Street the water drains westward to the same sump.

From Thirteenth Street the water drains eastward to a sump well at Fifth Street through a 12 inch terra cotta pipe to Eleventh Street; from here through a 15 inch terra cotta pipe under the north track. From the east portal the drainage is carried westward to the sump at Fifth Street.

There is placed between the rails of the express track a sump 2 feet wide and 3 feet long every 50 feet. These sumps connect to the terra cotta pipes before referred to. Where the tracks are on a grade, it was not necessary to make any special provision for drainage, but where the tracks are on a level, the cement finish is given a slope of 3 inches in 100 feet between the sumps.

Along the outside of the tracks there are small floor drains and 3 inch terra cotta pipes, which connect to the sumps to take care of the drainage water here.

The sump well at Twenty-second Street is 11 feet 3 inches wide by 9 feet 6 inches long, and has a capacity of about 5,800 gallons of water. The two centrifugal pumps are held by supports fastened to the bottom of the well. The motors are placed on the floor about 6 feet 8 inches above the bottom of the well.

There is very little drainage water at Fifteenth Street, and two sewage ejectors were installed to take care of this, as well as the toilet rooms. These sewage ejectors are in duplicate, each having a capacity of 200 gallons per minute. They operate by compressed air taken from the air line which supplies the air used for operating the signals.

At Thirteenth Street the pumps are placed in a dry well alongside the sump well, and the water is drawn from the wet well into the pumps through two 6 inch pipes passing through the intervening wall. The motors are placed on the level of the express platform, the shafts that connect to the pumps extending through the local platform and being encased in a sheet iron guard. The wet well, exclusive of the drains and sumps, has a capacity of 7,500 gallons of water.

The city sewer at the Fifth Street Station is above the level of the platform, so there were installed two Ansonia sewage ejectors to discharge the toilet room drainage into the sewer. Each has a capacity of 150 gallons per minute. The ejectors are operated by compressed air taken from the signal air line, and are placed in a pit next to the sump well at the east end of the Fifth Street Station.

The two pumps for drainage at this place are placed in a dry well, and take the water from the wet well through two 6 inch cast iron pipes built in the wall of the wet well. The wet well has a capacity of about 15,000 gallons. The motors are installed on the level of the Fifth Street platform, with shafts about 15 feet long extending down to the pumps. Motors and sewage ejectors are in a room specially built for their accommodation on the east end of the Fifth Street platform.

The pumps are all of 5 inch vertical shaft type with open bronze propellers and glands. Each pump is rated at 600 gallons per minute. They are direct connected to $12\frac{1}{2}$ horsepower Electro-Dynamic motors, of vertical shaft 550 volt 815 revolution direct current interpole type. They are operated by Cutler-Hammer floats and tank switches, and Cutler-Hammer Bulletin 70 automatic starters.

The power for operating the pump motors is taken from the direct current Subway lighting cable, but the wiring is so arranged that they can be connected to the third rail in case of trouble on the lighting cable.

T. B. McAvoy, *President*   John C. McAvoy, *Secretary and General Manager*

The McAvoy Vitrified Brick Co.

Offices: Rooms 2, 3 and 4
German-American Building
Philadelphia

Annual Capacity, 15,000,000

Vitrified Bricks and Blocks for Streets and Roadways

Vitrified Invert Bricks for Sewers and Tunnels

We furnished all Bricks used in the Subway

BRIDGES

MAIN OFFICE AND SHOP
22d St. and Washington Ave.
Philadelphia, Pa.

BRIDGE SHOP
EDDYSTONE, PA.

BRANCH OFFICES
1622 Real Estate Bldg.
Philadelphia, Pa.

No. 1 W. 34th St.
New York

BUILDINGS

BELMONT IRON WORKS

ENGINEERS AND CONTRACTORS

Structural Steel and Ornamental Iron

FOR

Bridges and Buildings

TANK TOWERS

CONTRACTORS FOR
Elevated Stations
Philadelphia
Rapid Transit Co.

Railroad Bridges
Highway "
Draw "
Locomotive Turntables
Office and Mill Buildings
Tank Towers
ORNAMENTAL IRON
Bridge Railings
Stairs and Grilles
Beams, Angles and Plates
of all sizes
carried in stock

ORNAMENTAL WORK

BOND, $800,000

THIS Company, with its associate companies, executed the contractors' bond in the sum of $800,000 for the Millard Construction Company, guaranteeing the completion of this magnificent piece of work, which is a monument to the enterprise of those connected with the Philadelphia Rapid Transit Company and the Millard Construction Company.

National Surety Co. of New York
Wm. B. Joyce, President

The Thos. B. Smith Company
General Agent
BETZ BUILDING
PHILADELPHIA

Smith Mixer

Equipped with Batch Loading Device

Smith Mixers were used on the Philadelphia Subway, giving excellent satisfaction to both engineer and contractor

SEND FOR CATALOGUE

Contractors' Supply and Equipment Co.
Consolidated with The T. L. Smith Co.

NEW YORK OFFICE:	CHICAGO OFFICE:	MILWAUKEE OFFICE:
170 BROADWAY	OLD COLONY BUILDING	MAJESTIC BUILDING

American Bridge Company of New York

Engineers and Contractors for Structural Steel for Every Purpose

Annual capacity 750,000 tons

Contracting Offices in Twenty-four American Cities

Philadelphia Office — Pennsylvania Building

GENERAL OFFICES

Hudson Terminal, 30 Church Street

NEW YORK

Vulcanite Portland Cement

Trade-Mark Registered U. S. Patent Office

250,000 Barrels

used in the construction of the Market Street Elevated and Subway of the Philadelphia Rapid Transit Company

LAND TITLE BUILDING
PHILADELPHIA

FLAT IRON BUILDING
NEW YORK

Westinghouse

STEAM TURBINES

A 25,000 H. P. Turbine

Manufactured by the Westinghouse Machine Co., the pioneers and leaders in the development of this modern prime mover.

Over a million horse-power in daily operation

Special types are built for non-condensing service; for utilizing exhaust steam and for driving centrifugal pumps, blowers, etc.

The Company also builds **LEBLANC CONDENSERS**, especially designed to insure the high vacuum desirable in steam turbine operation.

The Westinghouse Machine Co.
Steam Turbines, Steam Engines, Gas Engines, Gas Producers, Storage Batteries and the Roney Stoker

New York City, 165 Broadway
Boston, 131 State St.
Cleveland, New England Building
Chicago, 171 La Salle St.

Cincinnati, Traction Building
Atlanta, Candler Building
St. Louis, Chemical Building
Pittsburg, Westinghouse Building

Philadelphia, North American Building
Denver, M. Phee Building
San Francisco, Hunt, Mirk & Co.

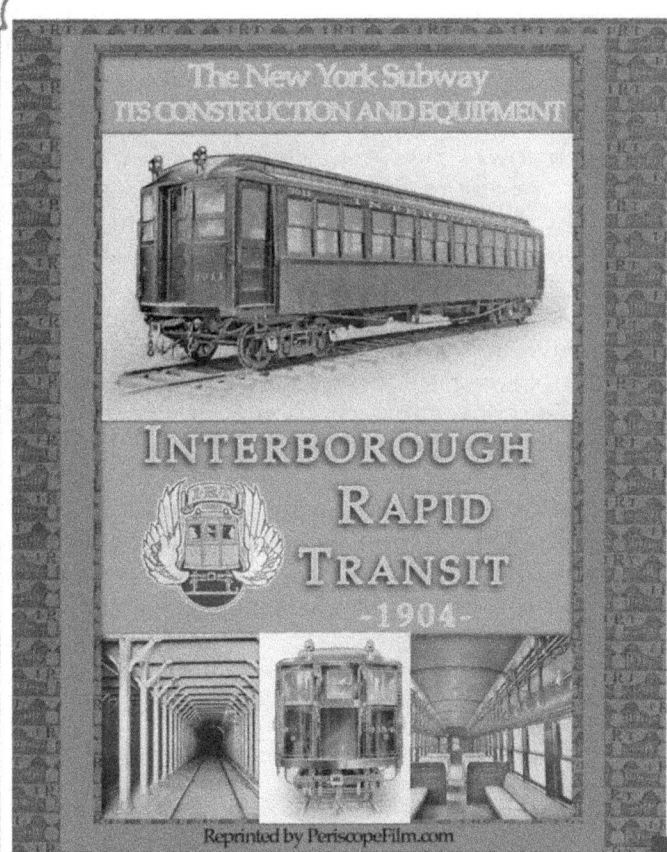

On October 27, 1904, the Interborough Rapid Transit Company opened the first subway in New York City. Running between City Hall and 145th Street at Broadway, the line was greeted with enthusiasm and, in some circles, trepidation. Created under the supervision of Chief Engineer S.L.F. Deyo, the arrival of the IRT foreshadowed the end of the "elevated" transit era on the island of Manhattan. The subway proved such a success that the IRT Co. soon achieved a monopoly on New York public transit. In 1940 the IRT and its rival the BMT were taken over by the City of New York. Today, the IRT subway lines still exist, primarily in Manhattan where they are operated as the "A Division" of the subway. Reprinted here is a special book created by the IRT, recounting the design and construction of the fledgling subway system. Originally created in 1904, it presents the IRT story with a flourish, and with numerous fascinating illustrations and rare photographs.

Originally written in the late 1900's and then periodically revised, A History of the Baldwin Locomotive Works chronicles the origins and growth of one of America's greatest industrial-era corporations. Founded in the early 1830's by Philadelphia jeweler Matthais Baldwin, the company built a huge number of steam locomotives before ceasing production in 1949. These included the 4-4-0 American type, 2-8-2 Mikado and 2-8-0 Consolidation. Hit hard by the loss of the steam engine market, Baldwin soldiered on for a brief while, producing electric and diesel engines. General Electric's dominance of the market proved too much, and Baldwin finally closed its doors in 1956. By that time over 70,500 Baldwin locomotives had been produced. This high quality reprint of the official company history dates from 1920. The book has been slightly reformatted, but care has been taken to preserve the integrity of the text.

NOW AVAILABLE AT WWW.PERISCOPEFILM.COM

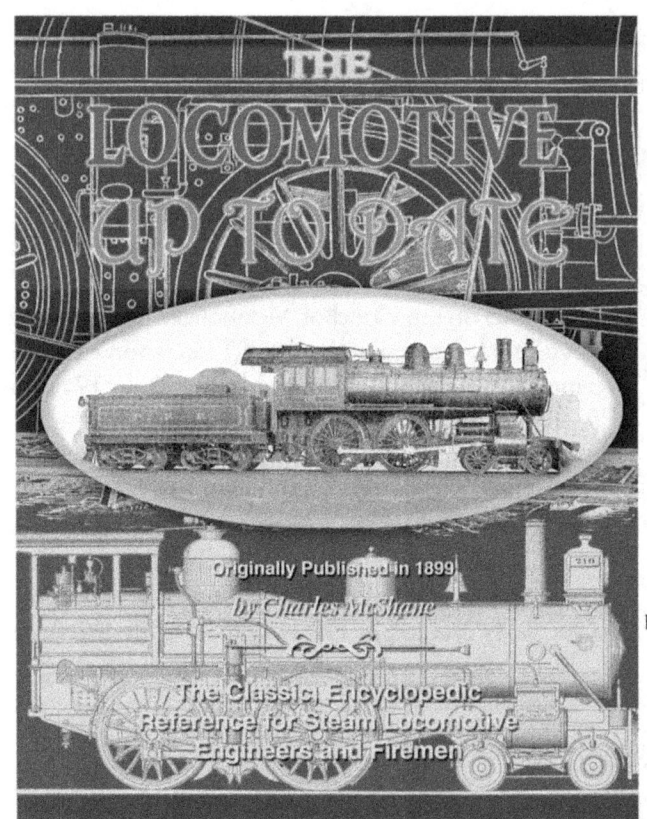

When it was originally published in 1899, **The Locomotive Up to Date** was hailed as "...the most definitive work ever published concerning the mechanism that has transformed the American nation: the steam locomotive." Filled with over 700 pages of text, diagrams and photos, this remains one of the most important railroading books ever written. From steam valves to sanders, trucks to side rods, it's a treasure trove of information, explaining in easy-to-understand language how the most sophisticated machines of the 19th Century were operated and maintained. This new edition is an exact duplicate of the original. Reformatted as an easy-to-read 8.5x11 volume, it's delightful for railroad enthusiasts of all ages.

Originally printed in 1898 and then periodically revised, The Motorman...and His Duties served as the definitive training text for a generation of streetcar operators. A must-have for the trolley or train enthusiast, it is also an important source of information for museum staff and docents. Lavishly illustrated with numerous photos and black and white line drawings, this affordable reprint contains all of the original text. Includes chapters on trolley car types and equipment, troubleshooting, brakes, controllers, electricity and principles, electric traction, multi-car control and has a convenient glossary in the back. If you've ever operated a trolley car, or just had an electric train set, this is a terrific book for your shelf!

ALSO NOW AVAILABLE FROM PERISCOPEFILM.COM!

THE CLASSIC 1911 TROLLEY CAR BUILDER'S REFERENCE BOOK

ELECTRIC RAILWAY DICTIONARY

By Rodney Hitt
Associate Editor, Electric Railway Journal

REPRINTED BY PERISCOPEFILM.COM

©2008-2010 Periscope Film LLC
All Rights Reserved
ISBN#978-1-935700-26-5
www.PeriscopeFilm.com

www.ingramcontent.com/pod-product-compliance
Lightning Source LLC
LaVergne TN
LVHW061345060426
835512LV00012B/2573